# Simple Solutions.
## Minutes a Day-Mastery for a Lifetime!

# Common Core Mathematics 4

Nancy L. McGraw         Christopher Backs
Donna M. Mazzola        Diane Dillon
Nancy Tondy             Lori Lender

Bright Ideas Press, LLC
Cleveland, OH

# Simple Solutions
## Common Core Mathematics 4

**Printed in the United States of America**

The writers of *Simple Solutions* Common Core Mathematics aligned the series in accordance with information from the following:

National Governors Association Center for Best Practices, Council of Chief State School Officers. *Common Core State Standards, Mathematics.* Washington, D.C.: National Governors Association Center for Best Practices, Council of Chief State School Officers, 2010.

United States coin images from the United States Mint.

ISBN: 978-1-60873-318-7

*Cover Design*: Dan Mazzola
*Editors*: Rebecca Toukonen
Randy Reetz

Copyright © 2015 by Bright Ideas Press, LLC
Cleveland, Ohio

# *Welcome!*

# Simple Solutions.

## Minutes a Day-Mastery for a Lifetime!

*Dear Student:*

*This workbook will give you the opportunity to practice skills you have learned in previous grades. By practicing these skills each day, you will gain confidence in your math ability.*

*Using this workbook will help you understand math concepts more easily. For many of you, using Simple Solutions will give you a more positive attitude towards math in general.*

*In order for this program to help you be successful, it is extremely important that you do a lesson every day. It is also important that you check your answers and ask your teacher for help with the problems you didn't understand or that you did incorrectly.*

*Simple Solutions: Minutes a day—Mastery for a Lifetime!*

 *When you are finished with this book, please recycle it if you can.*

# Lesson #1

1.  $475 + 869 = ?$

2.  Round 47 to the nearest ten.

3.  The shelf could hold 224 kilograms of books.   The students placed 179 kilograms of books on the shelf.  How many more kilograms could the shelf hold?

4.  Fill in the sign to make this sentence true.   656 ◯ 566

5.  $30 - 16 = ?$

6.  A rectangle has 2 pairs of parallel sides.  The distance around the outside of a rectangle is the perimeter.  Find the perimeter.

7.  Count by 5s.   25, 30, 35, _____, _____, 50

8.  $4 \times 8 = ?$

9.  Find the area of the rectangle.

10. $36 \div 9 = ?$

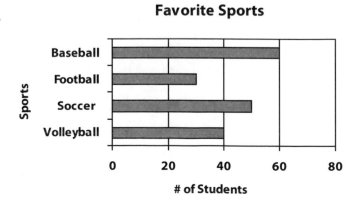

11. Travis drank 48 glasses of water.  If he drank 8 glasses a day, how many days did it take for him to drink all 48 glasses?

12. What time will it be 15 minutes after 10:30?

13. **In expanded form, the number 678 is written 600 + 70 + 8.** Write 435 in expanded form.

Use the graph to answer questions 14 – 15.

14. Write the number who prefer
    A) soccer     B) football

15. How many students prefer baseball over volleyball?

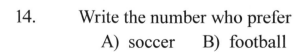

**Favorite Sports**

(Bar graph showing # of Students for each sport:)
- Baseball: 60
- Football: 30
- Soccer: 50
- Volleyball: 40

Sports (y-axis)  /  # of Students (x-axis: 0, 20, 40, 60, 80)

| 1.      4.NBT.4 | 2.      4.NBT.3 | 3.      3.MD.2 |
|---|---|---|
| 4.      4.NBT.2 | 5.      4.NBT.4 | 6.      3.MD.8 <br><br> 6 ft <br> 10 ft |
| 7.      2.NBT.2 | 8.      3.OA.7 | 9.      3.MD.7 <br> 5 inches <br> 3 inches |
| 10.      3.OA.7 | 11.      3.OA.3 | 12.      3.MD.1 |
| 13.      4.NBT.2 | 14.      2.MD.10 | 15.      2.MD.10 |

# Lesson #2

1.      $8 \times 3 = ?$

2.      Find the area.

3.      Round 279 to the nearest hundred.

4.      Write 537 in words.

5.      Fill in the sign to make this sentence true.      $900 \bigcirc 890$

6.      Write the base-ten number for $400 + 50 + 1$.

7.      $465 + 378 = ?$

8.      Draw along the dotted lines to divide the rectangle.  Shade in one part.  What fraction is shaded?

9.      $80 \times 7 = ?$

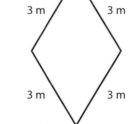

3 m          3 m

3 m          3 m

10.     Find the perimeter of the rhombus.

11.     $56 \div 7 = ?$

12.     Mrs. Jones worked a total of 63 hours.  She worked 7 hours each day.  For how many days did she work?

13.     Show the distributive property when solving $6 \times 9$.

        $6 \times (4 + 5) = ($_____ $\times$ _____$) + ($_____ $\times$ _____$) = $ _____ $+$ _____ $= 54$

14.     $832 - 265 = ?$

15.     After a week of sunshine, 24 tomatoes ripened on the vines.  There were 3 ripe tomatoes on each vine. How many tomato vines were there in all?  Write a division sentence to show the problem.

        _____ $\div$ _____ $=$ _____

| 1.          3.OA.7 | 2.          3.MD.7 | 3.          4.NBT.3 |
|---|---|---|
|  | 9 cm<br>4 cm |  |
| 4.          4.NBT.2 | 5.          4.NBT.2 | 6.          4.NBT.2 |
| 7.          4.NBT.4 | 8.          3.G.2 | 9.          3.NBT.3 |
| 10.         3.MD.8 | 11.         3.OA.7 | 12.         3.OA.3 |
| 13.         3.OA.5 | 14.         4.NBT.4 | 15.         3.OA.3 |

# Lesson #3

1.  The charity gave 352 kilograms of food to earthquake victims the day after an earthquake and another 521 kilograms of food the second day. How many more kilograms of food were given the second day than the first day?

2.  What fraction of the hexagon is shaded?

3.  $9 + \underline{\quad} = 18$

4.  Calculate the perimeter and area of the rectangle.

5.  $600 - 241 = ?$

6.  Paul came to bat 8 times in each of 4 games. Paul got on base or was out 24 times. The rest were home runs. How many home runs did Paul hit? Write two number sentences. Then solve for $x$.

7.  What is the answer to a multiplication problem called?

8.  Trina must spend at least 25 minutes practicing her piano. If she starts at 6:25 p.m., what is the earliest time she can finish?

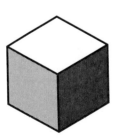

9.  Round 845 to the nearest hundred.

10. $937 + 258 = ?$

11. Which picture shows 8 as $48 \div 6$?

12. Give the name of the shape shown to the right.

13. $6 \times 6 = ?$

14. $32 \div 4 = ?$

15. $6 \times 8 = ?$

| 1. 3.MD.2 | 2. 3.G.2 | 3. 3.NBT.2 |
|---|---|---|
| | | |
| 4. 3.MD.8 <br><br> 9 in. <br> 2 in. [rectangle] | 5. 4.NBT.4 | 6. 3.OA.8 |
| 7. 3.OA.7 | 8. 3.MD.1 | 9. 4.NBT.3 |
| 10. 4.NBT.4 | 11. 3.OA.3 <br><br> | 12. 2.G.1 |
| 13. 3.OA.7 | 14. 3.OA.7 | 15. 3.OA.7 |

# Lesson #4

1.    A one hour TV show has 22 minutes of commercials.  How many minutes are left for the show?

2.    $46 - 12 = ?$

3.    $7 \times 9 = ?$

4.    $54 \div 6 = ?$

5.    $37 + 56 + 13 = ?$

6.    Find the perimeter of the square.

7.    $60 \times 6 = ?$

8.    The art students bought 28 kilograms of gourds for their projects on Monday. They didn't have enough so they bought 37 kilograms of gourds on Tuesday. How many kilograms of gourds did they buy altogether?

9.    Round 586 to the nearest hundred.

10.   Draw a square and divide it into six equal parts.  Shade in $\frac{1}{6}$ of it.

11.   $652 - 375 = ?$

12.   Layla sorted her hair clips by color.  She had 6 colors and 5 clips of each color. She decided to give 8 of the clips to her twin sister.  How many of the clips did she keep?  Write two number sentences.  Then solve for $x$.

13.   Show the distributive property when solving $5 \times 7$.
      $5 \times (4 + 3) = ($ \_\_\_\_ $\times$ \_\_\_\_ $) + ($ \_\_\_\_ $\times$ \_\_\_\_ $) = $ \_\_\_\_ $+$ \_\_\_\_ $=$ \_\_\_\_

14.   Fill in the sign to make this sentence true.     $3,786 \bigcirc 3,875$

15.   $16 +$ \_\_\_\_\_ $= 38$

| | | |
|---|---|---|
| **1.**      3.MD.1 | **2.**      4.NBT.4 | **3.**      3.OA.7 |
| **4.**      3.OA.7 | **5.**      2.NBT.6 | **6.**      3.MD.8 <br><br> 4 in. |
| **7.**      3.NBT.3 | **8.**      3.MD.2 | **9.**      4.NBT.3 |
| **10.**      3.G.2 | **11.**      4.NBT.4 | **12.**      3.OA.8 |
| **13.**      3.OA.5 | **14.**      4.NBT.2 | **15.**      4.NBT.4 |

# Lesson #5

1.    Draw along the dotted lines to divide the hexagon.
      Shade in one part.  What fraction is shaded?

2.    Ten ones are equal to one ten.  $(10 \times 1 = 10)$
      Ten tens $(10 \times 10)$ are equal to one _____.

3.    Round 813 to the nearest hundred.

4.    Fill in the sign to make this sentence true.    2,439 $\bigcirc$ 2,493

5.    The store mailed out 710 kilograms of packages during the first week of the
      holiday season.  The last week, they mailed out 519 kilograms of packages.
      How many kilograms less did they mail out the last week than the first?

6.    **The multiplication sentence 15 = 3 × 5 means 15 is 3 times as many as 5,
      and 15 is 5 times as many as 3.**
      Fill in the missing number.  16 is _____ times as many as 2.

7.    $50 \div 10 = ?$

8.    Find the area of the rectangle.

9.    **A point has no length or width.  It is named with a capital letter.**
      There is a point in the box.  Label it A.

10.   Write $2,000 + 400 + 30 + 1$ in base-ten numerals.

11.   Giovanni called his dad at 4:15, and his dad said, "Call me back in 10 minutes."
      What time should Giovanni call back?

12.   Heather sorted 72 cans of juice by type.  She had equal amounts of 8 different
      kinds of juice.  How many cans of each kind did Heather have?  Write a division
      sentence to show the problem.    _____ ÷ _____ = _____

13.   $5 \times 4 = ?$

14.   Each side is the same length.  What is the length of each missing side?

15.   $46 + 59 = ?$

| 1.      3.G.2 | 2.      4.NBT.1 | 3.      4.NBT.3 |
|---|---|---|
| | | |
| **4.**      4.NBT.2 | **5.**      3.MD.2 | **6.**      4.OA.1 |
| | | |
| **7.**      3.OA.7 | **8.**      3.MD.7 <br> 4 m <br> 7 m | **9.**      4.G.1 |
| | | |
| **10.**      4.NBT.2 | **11.**      3.MD.1 | **12.**      3.OA.3 |
| | | |
| **13.**      3.OA.7 | **14.**      3.MD.8 <br> perimeter: <br> 36 in. | **15.**      3.NBT.2 |
| | | |

# Lesson #6

1.      $6 \times 7 = ?$

2.      Round 87 to the nearest ten.

3.      $365 + 249 = ?$

4.      $842 - 191 = ?$

5.      What is the answer to a division problem called?

6.      $19 + \underline{\quad\quad} = 41$

7.      It takes 18 minutes to walk from home to the market.  If Lisa leaves the house at 2:20, what time will she get to the market?

8.      Write 3,763 in expanded form.

9.      Fill in the missing numbers:  42 is _____ times as many as 7, and it is 7 times as many as _____.

10.     Find the area of the square.

11.     $5 \times \underline{\quad\quad} = 35$

12.     Which of these is a point?  Draw it in the answer box.      ᴜ    ●    ᴧ

13.     $30 \div 5 = ?$

14.     What is the length of side C?

15.     Fill in the sign to make this sentence true.      1,474 ◯ 1,744

| 1.    3.OA.7 | 2.    4.NBT.3 | 3.    4.NBT.4 |
|---|---|---|
| 4.    4.NBT.4 | 5.    3.OA.7 | 6.    3.NBT.2 |
| 7.    3.MD.1 | 8.    4.NBT.2 | 9.    4.OA.1 |
| 10.    3.MD.7 <br><br> 6 cm | 11.    3.OA.4 | 12.    4.G.1 |
| 13.    3.OA.7 | 14.    3.MD.8 <br><br> 6 cm    C <br> perimeter: 37 cm <br> 7 cm    5 cm <br> 7 cm | 15.    4.NBT.2 |

# Lesson #7

1.  Tonya jogs 5 miles each week.  If she did this for 8 weeks, how many miles would Tonya jog?

2.  Round 31 to the nearest ten.

3.  $372 - 199 = ?$

4.  What is the answer to a multiplication problem called?

5.  Ten tens are equal to one hundred.  $(10 \times 10 = 100)$
    Ten hundreds $(10 \times 100)$ are equal to one _____.

6.  Fill in the sign to make this sentence true.    $31,816 \bigcirc 30,976$

7.  Write the base-ten number for $5,000 + 20 + 3$.

8.  Fill in the missing numbers:  45 is _____ times as many as 9, and it is 9 times as many as _____.

9.  The bookstore mailed out 7 copies of a bestseller that weighed 2 kilograms.  In all, how much did the packages weigh?

10. $42 \div 7 = ?$

11. Courtney hit 30 home runs during the baseball tournament.  If she hit 3 homeruns in each game, how many games did Courtney play in?  Write a division sentence to show the problem.    _____ $\div$ _____ $=$ _____

12. $700 - 454 = ?$

13. Find the area.

14. $8 \times 8 = ?$

15. **One foot (ft) is 12 inches (in.).**  Write 1 ft = 12 in. in the box.

| | | |
|---|---|---|
| **1.**    3.OA.3 | **2.**    4.NBT.3 | **3.**    4.NBT.4 |
| **4.**    3.OA.7 | **5.**    4.NBT.1 | **6.**    4.NBT.2 |
| **7.**    4.NBT.2 | **8.**    4.OA.1 | **9.**    3.MD.2 |
| **10.**    3.OA.7 | **11.**    3.OA.3 | **12.**    4.NBT.4 |
| **13.**    3.MD.7 <br> 8 ft, 7 ft square | **14.**    3.OA.7 | **15.**    4.MD.1 |

# Lesson #8

1.  Round 31 to the nearest ten.

2.  $312 - 178 = ?$

3.  $568 + 179 = ?$

4.  $15 \div 5 = ?$

5.  Each art student received a 4 kilogram ball of clay. If there were 8 students, how much did the balls of clay weigh altogether?

6.  Fill in the sign to make this sentence true.   8,479 $\bigcirc$ 8,794

7.  Compare the shaded parts of the two rectangles. Choose <, =, or >.

8.  One foot (ft) equals _____ inches (in.).

9.  $40 \div 8 = ?$

10. Find the area.

11. Write 4,362 using words.

12. What is the length of the other two sides of the rectangle?

13. Draw a point.

14. Divide the rectangle into three equal parts. Shade in one part. What fraction of the rectangle is shaded in?

15. Altogether, a group of girls biked around the block 32 times. Each girl biked around the block the same number of times. If there were 4 girls, how many times did each girl bike around the block? Write a division sentence to show the problem.

| | | |
|---|---|---|
| **1.** 4.NBT.3 | **2.** 4.NBT.4 | **3.** 4.NBT.4 |
| **4.** 3.OA.7 | **5.** 3.MD.2 | **6.** 4.NBT.2 |
| **7.** 3.NF.3 4/6 ◯ 2/3 | **8.** 4.MD.1 | **9.** 3.OA.7 |
| **10.** 3.MD.7 | **11.** 4.NBT.2 | **12.** 3.MD.8 |
| **13.** 4.G.1 | **14.** 3.G.2 | **15.** 3.OA.3 |

# Lesson #9

1.  Jeff started his test at 8:30. He finished the test at 10:00.
    How long did it take him to complete his test?

2.  If 1 ft = 12 in., then 2 ft = _____ in.

3.  _____ × 6 = 48

4.  Find the area.

5.  20 × 7 = ?

6.  What is the length of the missing side of the quadrilateral?

7.  3,465 + 4,786 = _____

8.  Fill in the sign to make this sentence true.  5,816 ◯ 7,582

9.  Write the number *four thousand, seven hundred thirty-six* as a base-ten
    number.

10. Fill in a number to make the fractions equal.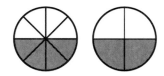

11. Round 6,745 to the nearest thousand.

12. **A line has no endpoints.  It goes forever in two directions.**
    Draw a line.  Mark point A and point B along the line.   A        B
    Say, "line AB" or "line BA."

13. Ten tens are equal to one hundred.  (10 × 10 = 100)
    Ten hundreds (10 × 100) are equal to one _____.

14. 4,000 − 1,836 = ?

15. Fill in the missing numbers:  32 is _____ times as many as 4,
    and it is 4 times as many as _____.

| 1. 3.MD.1 | 2. 4.MD.1 | 3. 3.OA.4 |
|---|---|---|
| | | |

| 4. 3.MD.7 | 5. 3.NBT.3 | 6. 3.MD.8 |
|---|---|---|
| 6 ft, 6 ft (square) | | z, perimeter: 58 cm, 18 cm, 16 cm, 8 cm |

| 7. 4.NBT.4 | 8. 4.NBT.2 | 9. 4.NBT.2 |
|---|---|---|
| | | |

| 10. 3.NF.3 | 11. 4.NBT.3 | 12. 4.G.1 |
|---|---|---|
| $\dfrac{\Box}{8} = \dfrac{2}{4}$ | | |

| 13. 4.NBT.1 | 14. 4.NBT.4 | 15. 4.OA.1 |
|---|---|---|
| | | |

# Lesson #10

1. Mrs. Hong travels 189 miles the first week, 224 miles the second week, and 91 miles the third week. Is her total more than or less than 500 miles? Estimate by rounding to the **highest place value**.

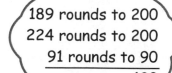

189 rounds to 200
224 rounds to 200
91 rounds to 90
490

2. Round 6,541 to the nearest thousand.

3. $3 \times 6 = ?$

4. $28 \div 7 = ?$

5. $3,920 + 4,574 = ?$

6. $20 \times 4 = ?$

7. Fill in the sign to make this sentence true.   $3,425 \bigcirc 9,286$

8. Laura sold 3 tickets to each of 4 classmates. How many tickets did she sell?

9. Write 4,323 in expanded form.

10. Draw a line.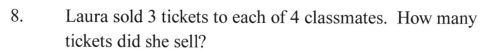

11. Simon jumped 1 foot. How many inches did he jump?

12. It is 2:15 p.m. now. What time was it three hours ago?

13. **Tom ordered a whole pizza. One-half of the pizza has mushrooms. If the whole pizza is divided into four equal parts, it looks like two-fourths of the pizza has mushrooms. If that whole pizza is divided into eight equal parts, it looks like four-eighths of the pizza has mushrooms.**

    **The amounts $\frac{1}{2}$, $\frac{2}{4}$, and $\frac{4}{8}$ are called equivalent fractions.**

    Write *equivalent* in the box.

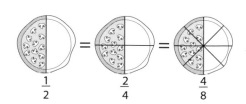

$\frac{1}{2}$      $\frac{2}{4}$      $\frac{4}{8}$

14. $3,850 - 1,575 = ?$

15. Fill in a number to make the fractions equal.

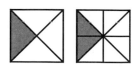

| 1.      4.OA.3<br><br>A) more than 500<br><br>B) less than 500<br><br>C) answer not given | 2.      4.NBT.3 | 3.      3.OA.7 |
|---|---|---|
| 4.      3.OA.7 | 5.      4.NBT.4 | 6.      3.NBT.3 |
| 7.      4.NBT.2 | 8.      3.OA.3 | 9.      4.NBT.2 |
| 10.      4.G.1 | 11.      4.MD.1 | 12.      3.MD.1 |
| 13.      4.NF.1 | 14.      4.NBT.4 | 15.      3.NF.3 <br><br> $\dfrac{1}{\square} = \dfrac{2}{8}$ |

# Lesson #11

1.    In all, the dogs performed 48 tricks at the dog show. If each dog performed 6 tricks, how many dogs performed tricks? Write a division sentence to show the problem.

2.    $4 \times 9 = ?$

3.    Fill in each number to make the fractions equal.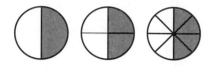

4.    $56 \div 7 = ?$

5.    Toya saved $198 in December, $342 in January, and $277 in February. Did she save more or less than $700? (Estimate by rounding to the highest place value. Check the *Help Pages* if you are not sure how to do this.)

6.    $2{,}634 - 459 = ?$

7.    Draw a rectangle with four sides of equal length.

8.    Ten hundreds equal one thousand. $(10 \times 100 = 1{,}000)$
      Ten times one thousand $(10 \times 1{,}000)$ is equal to one _____.

9.    **One yard (yd) is 3 feet (ft).** Write 1 yd = 3 ft in the box.

10.   Fill in the missing numbers: 63 is _____ times as many as 7, and it is 7 times as many as _____.

11.   $6{,}839 \bigcirc 4{,}777$

12.   $9{,}000 - 3{,}629 = ?$

13.   Find the area.

14.   $30 \times 2 = ?$

15.   **A line segment has end points. Say, "line segment MN" or**    M•————•N
      **"line segment NM."** Four line segments form the rectangle:
      $\overline{MN}, \overline{NP}, \overline{OP}$, and _____. Write the missing line segment.

| | | |
|---|---|---|
| **1.**    3.OA.3 | **2.**    3.OA.7 | **3.**    3.NF.3 $$\frac{1}{2} = \frac{\Box}{4} \quad \frac{1}{2} = \frac{\Box}{8}$$ |
| **4.**    3.OA.7 | **5.**    4.OA.3 | **6.**    4.NBT.4 |
| **7.**    3.G.1 | **8.**    4.NBT.1 | **9.**    4.MD.1 |
| **10.**    4.OA.1 | **11.**    4.NBT.2 | **12.**    4.NBT.4 |
| **13.**    3.MD.7 <br> 3 cm <br> 8 cm | **14.**    3.NBT.3 | **15.**    4.G.1 |

# Lesson #12

1. $4,209 - 2,165 = ?$

2. Max packed 10 boxes of clothes for his move to a new city. Each box weighed 7 kilograms. How many kilograms did the boxes weigh altogether?

3. $50 \times 5 = ?$

4. Round 4,892 to the nearest thousand.

5. $24 \div 6 = ?$

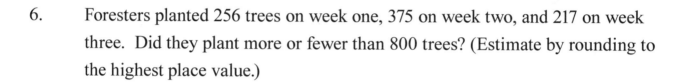

6. Foresters planted 256 trees on week one, 375 on week two, and 217 on week three. Did they plant more or fewer than 800 trees? (Estimate by rounding to the highest place value.)

7. $8 \times 9 = ?$

8. It is 12:20 p.m. now. What time was it 1 hour and 5 minutes ago?

9. One yard (yd) equals _____ feet (ft).

10. $2,436 + 1,988 = ?$

11. Draw a square and divide it into eight equal parts. Shade in $\frac{1}{8}$ of it.

12. $4,586 \bigcirc 9,674$

13. Carlos pitched 6 innings in each of 7 games. Erik pitched 33 innings. How many innings did they pitch altogether? Write two number sentences and solve for $x$.

14. $9 \times 6 = ?$

15. Draw a vertical line.

| | | |
|---|---|---|
| 1.  4.NBT.4 | 2.  3.MD.2 | 3.  3.NBT.3 |
| 4.  4.NBT.3 | 5.  3.OA.7 | 6.  4.OA.3 |
| 7.  3.OA.7 | 8.  3.MD.1 | 9.  4.MD.1 |
| 10.  4.NBT.4 | 11.  3.G.2 | 12.  4.NBT.2 |
| 13.  3.OA.8 | 14.  3.OA.7 | 15.  4.G.1 |

# Lesson #13

1.    $7,482 + 3,555 = ?$

2.    $7 \times 3 = ?$

3.    If 1 yd = 3 ft, then 2 yd = _____ ft.

4.    $30 \times 5 = ?$

5.    $8,000 - 2,877 = ?$

**Compatible Numbers**

🍎 $125 = 100 + 25$

🍋 $175 = 100 + 75$

🍊 $62 = 60 + 2$

🍐 $148 = 100 + 40 + 8$

Find numbers that are easy to add up.

6.    Yoder Farm delivered 125 apples, 148 pears, 175 peaches, and 62 melons last week.  If they deliver the same this week, how many pieces of fruit will the company have delivered in all?  (Use compatible numbers to find the exact total.)

7.    Fill in the missing numbers:  24 is _____ times as many as 8, and it is 8 times as many as _____.

8.    $32 \div 4 = ?$

9.    Round 2,931 to the nearest thousand.

10.   Devin read 8 books this summer.  That is 3 more than Austin read.  How many books did Austin read?  Choose the correct equation and solve it.

11.   Ten times one thousand is equal to one ten thousand.  $(10 \times 1,000 = 10,000)$  Ten times ten thousand $(10 \times 10,000)$ is equal to one _____.

12.   Draw a horizontal line.

13.   Fill in the unknown factor.  $7 \times$ _____ $= 63$

14.   $4,875 \bigcirc 6,785$

15.   All the models show $\frac{1}{2}$ shaded.  Write the equivalent names for the $\frac{1}{2}$ that are shown.

| 1. 4.NBT.4 | 2. 3.OA.7 | 3. 4.MD.1 |
|---|---|---|
| 4. 3.NBT.3 | 5. 4.NBT.4 | 6. 4.OA.3 |
| 7. 4.OA.1 | 8. 3.OA.7 | 9. 4.NBT.3 |
| 10. 4.OA.2<br><br>A) $b + 3 = 8$<br><br>B) $8 + 3 = b$ | 11. 4.NBT.1 | 12. 4.G.1 |
| 13. 3.OA.4 | 14. 4.NBT.2 | 15. 4.NF.1 |

# Lesson #14

1.  $7 \times 2 = ?$

2.  Write $8,000 + 400 + 30 + 7$ as a base-ten number.

3.  Use the distributive property to multiply $832 \times 3$.  Multiply 3 by all the values in $832$ $(800 + 30 + 2)$.  Show the product.

4.  Draw a line segment.

5.  $1,998 + 6,264 = ?$

6.  $20 \div 4 = ?$

7.  Write and solve a number sentence for *three times as many as 9.*

8.  Natalie swam 50 laps at the swim party.  That is 12 more laps than Sophia swam.  How many laps did Sophia swim?  Choose the correct equation and solve it.

9.  $40 \div 5 = ?$

10. **A line that goes on in one direction is a ray.**          F —————▶ G
    Draw a ray.  Label its endpoint F.

11. Ten times ten thousand is equal to one hundred thousand.
    $(10 \times 10,000 = 100,000)$  Ten times one hundred thousand $(10 \times 100,000)$
    is equal to one _____.

12. A garage housed 48 cars on Friday, 250 on Saturday, 152 on Sunday, and 50 on Monday.  Did they house more or fewer than 400 cars? (Use compatible numbers to find the exact total.)

13. The ribbon on the present was 36 inches long.  How many feet long was it?

14. $5,800 - 2,369 = ?$

15. All the models show $\frac{1}{2}$ shaded.  Write the
    equivalent names for the $\frac{1}{2}$ that are shown.

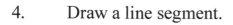

| | | |
|---|---|---|
| **1.** 3.OA.7 | **2.** 4.NBT.2 | **3.** 4.NBT.5 |
| **4.** 4.G.1 | **5.** 4.NBT.4 | **6.** 3.OA.7 |
| **7.** 4.OA.1 | **8.** 4.OA.2<br><br>A) $12 + 50 = s$<br><br>B) $12 + s = 50$ | **9.** 3.OA.7 |
| **10.** 4.G.1 | **11.** 4.NBT.1 | **12.** 4.OA.3 |
| **13.** 4.MD.1 | **14.** 4.NBT.4 | **15.** 4.NF.1 |

# Lesson #15

1.  Molly scored 4 goals at her soccer game. That is 3 more goals than she scored last week. How many goals did Molly score last week? Choose the correct equation and solve it.

2.  Round 5,767 to the nearest thousand.

3.  $7 \times 6 = ?$

4.  2,076 $\bigcirc$ 2,067

5.  $10,994 - 4,887 = ?$

6.  One yard (yd) is 36 inches (in.). Write 1 yd = 36 in. in the box.

7.  Write 3,281 using words.

8.  $2,456 + 9,873 = ?$

9.  Find the area.

10. $4 \times 25 = ?$ Use the distributive property. $4 \times (20 + 5)$

11. The Dollar Theater sold 102 tickets in April, 198 in May, 318 in June, and 182 in July. Did the theater serve more or fewer than 700 patrons? (Use compatible numbers before finding the exact total.)

12. Write and solve a number sentence for *six times as many as 4*.

13. Draw along the dotted lines to divide the square. Shade in one part. What fraction is shaded ?

14. All the models show $\frac{1}{2}$ shaded.
    Write the equivalent names for the $\frac{1}{2}$ that are shown.

15. Draw a ray.

| 1.    4.OA.2 <br><br> A) $3 + 4 = g$ <br><br> B) $g + 3 = 4$ | 2.    4.NBT.3 | 3.    3.OA.7 |
|---|---|---|
| 4.    4.NBT.2 | 5.    4.NBT.4 | 6.    4.MD.1 |
| 7.    4.NBT.2 | 8.    4.NBT.4 | 9.    3.MD.7 <br><br> 10 in. <br> ⬚ 2 in. |
| 10.    4.NBT.5 | 11.    4.OA.3 | 12.    4.OA.1 |
| 13.    3.G.2 <br><br> | 14.    4.NF.1 | 15.    4.G.1 |

# Lesson #16

1.  Write the fraction as a whole number.   $\dfrac{10}{1}$

2.  $9,858 - 6,439 = ?$

3.  The Dainty Dog groomed 147 dogs on Monday,  132 dogs on Tuesday, 251 dogs on Thursday, and 220 dogs on Friday.  Did they groom more or fewer than 800 dogs?

    For this one, round to the nearest ten; then use compatible numbers.

4.  Round 3,572 to the nearest hundred.

5.  Find the perimeter of the rectangle.

6.  $1,525 - 385 = ?$

7.  Find the area.

8.  $50 \times 7 = ?$

9.  Mary practiced her violin for 28 hours last week.  If she practiced for the same number of hours each day for 7 days, how many hours did she practice each day?

10.  One yard (yd) equals _____ inches (in.).

11.  Write and solve a number sentence for *eight times as many as 9.*

12.  Draw line segment $\overline{GH}$ .

13.  $17 \div 4 = ?$   (This answer will have a remainder.)

14.  Donavan has 23 video games in his collection.  That is 5 more than his friend, Carter, has.  How many games does Carter have in his collection? Choose the correct equation and solve it.

15.  $7,414 \bigcirc 6,404$

| 1.      3.NF.3 | 2.      4.NBT.4 | 3.      4.OA.3 |
|---|---|---|
| 4.      4.NBT.3 | 5.      3.MD.8<br><br>9 in.<br>2 in. [         ] | 6.      4.NBT.4 |
| 7.      3.MD.7<br><br>9 ft<br>[     ] 5 ft | 8.      3.NBT.3 | 9.      3.OA.3 |
| 10.      4.MD.1 | 11.      4.OA.1 | 12.      4.G.1 |
| 13.      3.OA.7 | 14.      4.OA.2<br><br>A) $5 + c = 23$<br><br>B) $5 + 23 = c$ | 15.      4.NBT.2 |

# Lesson #17

1. **Factor Pairs:** In $2 \times 3 = 6$, 2 and 3 are called factors and 6 is called the product. $3 \times 9 = 27$. Name the factors. What is the product?

2. Round 5,262 to the nearest thousand.

3. Use the distributive property to multiply $346 \times 4$. Multiply 4 by all the values in $346 (300 + 40 + 6)$. Show the product.

4. Draw a fraction model to show that $\frac{1}{2}$ and $\frac{3}{6}$ are equivalent.

5. $71,888 + 86,655 = ?$

6. **Factors are all of the whole numbers that can be divided exactly into a given number.** The factors of 6 are 1 and 6, 2 and 3. List the factors of 10.

7. Put these numbers in order from greatest to least.

   9,618       9,681       9,600

8. $452 - 197 = ?$

9. Draw a vertical line.

10. The zoo bought 93 pounds of peanuts for the elephants this month. That is 29 more pounds than they bought last month. How many peanuts did the zoo buy last month? Choose the correct equation and solve it.

11. Margie Thatcher filed 321 folders on Monday, 251 on Tuesday, 111 on Wednesday, and 201 on Thursday. Did she file more or fewer than 800 folders?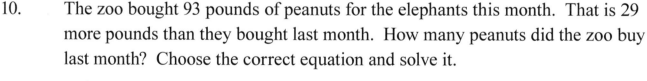

    Round to the highest place value.

12. Write and solve a number sentence for *three times as many as 8*.

13. If 1 yd = 36 in., then 2 yd = _____ in.

14. Write $6,000 + 400 + 20 + 7$ as a base-ten number.

15. Draw a point. Label it B.

| | | |
|---|---|---|
| **1.**         4.OA.4 | **2.**         4.NBT.3 | **3.**         4.NBT.5 |
| **4.**         4.NF.1 | **5.**         4.NBT.4 | **6.**         4.OA.4 |
| **7.**         4.NBT.2 | **8.**         4.NBT.4 | **9.**         4.G.1 |
| **10.**         4.OA.2 <br><br> A) $29 + p = 93$ <br><br> B) $29 + 93 = p$ | **11.**         4.OA.3 | **12.**         4.OA.1 |
| **13.**         4.MD.1 | **14.**         4.NBT.2 | **15.**         4.G.1 |

# Lesson #18

1. $7 \times 9 = ?$

2. Draw ray $\overrightarrow{ST}$ .

3. Find the rectangle's perimeter.

4. Find all the factor pairs for 18.

5. Use the distributive property to multiply 287 × 4. Multiply 4 by all the values in 287 (200 + 80 + 7). Show the product.

6. Ten times one hundred thousand is equal to one million. (10 × 100,000 = 1,000,000) A digit in one place represents _____ times what it represents in the place to its right.

7. $963 + 459 = ?$

8. Lauren has a fever. Her temperature is 101 degrees, which is 2 degrees higher than it was yesterday. What was Lauren's temperature yesterday? Choose the correct equation and solve it.

9. Amari has a piece of rope candy that is 1 foot long. She wants to share it equally with a friend. How many inches of candy will each girl get?

10. Find all the factor pairs for 24.

11. Round 4,231 to the nearest thousand.

12. $3,072 - 1,986 = ?$

13. Chef Duff baked a cake that was 36 inches tall. How many yards high was the cake?

14. Write and solve a number sentence for *seven times as many as 4*.

15. The Fancy Fish sold 347 cod sandwiches on Friday, 220 on Saturday, 148 on Sunday, and 180 on Monday. Did they sell more or fewer than 800 sandwiches?

| | | |
|---|---|---|
| **1.**　　3.OA.7 | **2.**　　4.G.1 | **3.**　　3.MD.8<br><br>6 cm<br>5 cm |
| **4.**　　4.OA.4 | **5.**　　4.NBT.5 | **6.**　　4.NBT.1 |
| **7.**　　4.NBT.4 | **8.**　　4.OA.2<br><br>A) $f + 2 = 101$<br><br>B) $101 + 2 = f$ | **9.**　　4.MD.2 |
| **10.**　　4.OA.4 | **11.**　　4.NBT.3 | **12.**　　4.NBT.4 |
| **13.**　　4.MD.1 | **14.**　　4.OA.1 | **15.**　　4.OA.3 |

# Lesson #19

1.      Leo rode his bike 4 feet before falling. How many inches did he ride his bike?

2.      $40 \div 9 = ?$ There will be a remainder.

3.      $6 \times 9 = ?$

4.      Draw line segment $\overline{BC}$.

5.      83,407 ◯ 83,470

6.      Find all the factor pairs for 16.

7.      All three sides of the triangle are the same length. Find the perimeter.

8.      Round 7,818 to the nearest thousand.

9.      $75,803 + 84,470 = ?$

10.      Madeline has 23 stickers in her collection. That is 17 more than her brother Max has in his collection. How many stickers does Max have in his collection? Choose the correct equation and solve it.

11.      Chad is a running back for his football team. He ran 7 yards during the game on Friday night. How many feet was that?

12.      $8,000 - 5,379 = ?$

13.      $752 \times 4 = ?$ Use the distributive property.
Multiply 4 by all the values in 752 $(700 + 50 + 2)$. Find the product.

14.      Compare the fractions. Find the fractions on each number line. The fraction that is farther to the right is greater.

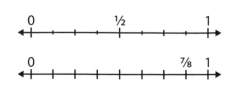

15.      Write and solve a number sentence for *four times as many as 3*.

| | | |
|---|---|---|
| **1.** 4.MD.1 | **2.** 3.OA.7 | **3.** 3.OA.7 |
| **4.** 4.G.1 | **5.** 4.NBT.2 | **6.** 4.OA.4 |
| **7.** 3.MD.8 12 m | **8.** 4.NBT.3 | **9.** 4.NBT.4 |
| **10.** 4.OA.2<br><br>A) $23 + 17 = s$<br><br>B) $17 + s = 23$ | **11.** 4.MD.2 | **12.** 4.NBT.4 |
| **13.** 4.NBT.5 | **14.** 4.NF.2<br><br>$\dfrac{1}{2} \bigcirc \dfrac{7}{8}$ | **15.** 4.OA.1 |

# Lesson #20

1.  $652 \times 5 = ?$

2.  Write and solve a number sentence for *eight times as many as 10.*

3.  John hit 15 home runs during his tournament baseball games this season. That is 9 more home runs than he hit last year. How many home runs did John hit last year? Choose the correct equation and solve it.

4.  $97,320 - 69,855 = ?$

5.  Find all the factor pairs for 24.

6.  $37 \div 6 = ?$ This answer will have a remainder.

7.  Draw a fraction model to show that $\frac{1}{2}$ and $\frac{4}{8}$ are equivalent.

8.  Draw line segment $\overline{JK}$.

9.  Winston the puppy ran 3 yards to get his ball. How many feet did he run?

10. Round 7,655 to the nearest thousand.

11. $8 \times 7 = ?$

12. Jayla walked 15 yards to her car on Monday and 9 yards to her car on Tuesday. How many yards did Jayla walk to her car over those two days? How many feet did she walk?

13. $43,325 \bigcirc 43,352$

14. Now that Alicia is at college, she uses a laundromat to do her laundry. She needs $8.00 worth of quarters each week. If she has 9 quarters saved, how many quarters does she need?

15. $42,766 + 38,723 = ?$

| 1.        4.NBT.5 | 2.        4.OA.1 | 3.        4.OA.2 |
|---|---|---|
| | | A) $9 + h = 15$<br><br>B) $15 + 9 = h$ |
| 4.        4.NBT.4 | 5.        4.OA.4 | 6.        3.OA.7 |
| | | |
| 7.        4.NF.1 | 8.        4.G.1 | 9.        4.MD.1 |
| | | |
| 10.        4.NBT.3 | 11.        3.OA.7 | 12.        4.MD.2 |
| | | |
| 13.        4.NBT.2 | 14.        4.MD.2 | 15.        4.NBT.4 |
| | | |

# Lesson #21

1.      Write 6,348 in expanded form.

2.      Use the distributive property to multiply 924 × 5.  Multiply 5 by all the values in 924 (900 + 20 + 4).  Show the product.

3.      76,816 + 42,396 = ?

4.      Together, Sally and Rachael ran 12 yards during a relay race.  Sally ran 15 feet of the distance.  How many feet did Rachael run?

5.      9,069 $\bigcirc$ 6,096

6.      Write and solve a number sentence for *three times as many as 25.*

7.      Compare the fractions.  Think about this: half of 8 is 4, so $\frac{4}{8} = \frac{1}{2}$.  Which has more eighths, $\frac{3}{8}$ or $\frac{4}{8}$?  That will help you know which is greater.

8.      **A prime number is a number with exactly 2 factors (the number itself and 1).  7 has factors of only 1 and 7.  7 is a prime number.**
        Is 11 a prime number?

9.      2 × 9 = ?

10.     During the first half of the week, Drew Burr picked 210 flowers.  During the second half, he picked half that many.  About how many total flowers did he pick, 300, 350, or 400?

11.     6,000 − 2,465 = ?

12.     Round 7,843 to the nearest hundred.

13.     Volunteers packed 36 boxes on Friday.  That is 3 times as many as they packed on Monday.  Choose the correct equation and use it to find how many boxes were packed on Monday.

14.     Tommy put out seeds for the birds.  He placed them in a straight line that was 2 yards long.  How many feet of seed did Tommy put out?

15.     **Two rays that share the same endpoint form an angle.  The end point is called a vertex.**  Angle BAT ($\angle BAT$), angle TAB ($\angle TAB$), and angle A ($\angle A$) each name the angle to the right.  Draw it in your box.

| | | |
|---|---|---|
| **1.** 4.NBT.2 | **2.** 4.NBT.5 | **3.** 4.NBT.4 |
| **4.** 4.MD.2 | **5.** 4.NBT.2 | **6.** 4.OA.1 |
| **7.** 4.NF.2 $$\frac{3}{8} \bigcirc \frac{1}{2}$$ | **8.** 4.OA.4 | **9.** 3.OA.7 |
| **10.** 4.OA.3 | **11.** 4.NBT.4 | **12.** 4.NBT.3 |
| **13.** 4.OA.2 A) $3 \times 36 = c$ B) $3 \times c = 36$ | **14.** 4.MD.1 | **15.** 4.G.1 |

# Lesson #22

1.  Margaret's rose bush has 48 flowers on it. That is 8 times as many as it had last week. Choose the best equation and use it to find how many flowers were on her rose bush last week.

2.  Find all the factor pairs for 20.

3.  Draw point $R$.

4.  $2,431 - 986 = ?$

5.  $25 \div 6 = ?$

6.  $86,412 \bigcirc 68,986$

7.  $5,000 = 500 \times$ _____

8.  Katie Lang spent $333 the first week, $220 the second week, $132 the third week, and $80 the fourth week. Did she spend more or less than $600?

9.  Round 46,313 to the nearest ten thousand.

10. **A right angle makes a square corner.**

    **It measures 90 degrees.** Draw a right angle.

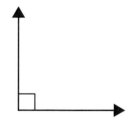

11. Which shows the use of the distributive property for $274 \times 6$?

12. Bob had a leash for his dog that was 3.5 feet long. How many inches was the leash?

13. Draw a fraction model to show that $\frac{1}{2}$ and $\frac{4}{8}$ are equivalent.

14. Write and solve a number sentence for *five times as many as 7.*

15. **Angles are formed wherever two rays share a common endpoint.**
    Draw the angle that is formed where $\overrightarrow{BC}$ and $\overrightarrow{BD}$ share a common endpoint.

| | | |
|---|---|---|
| **1.** 4.OA.2<br><br>A) $8 \times 48 = r$<br><br>B) $8 \times r = 48$ | **2.** 4.OA.4 | **3.** 4.G.1 |
| **4.** 4.NBT.4 | **5.** 3.OA.7 | **6.** 4.NBT.2 |
| **7.** 4.NBT.1 | **8.** 4.OA.3 | **9.** 4.NBT.3 |
| **10.** 4.G.1 | **11.** 4.NBT.5<br><br>A) $(20 \times 6) + (70 \times 6) + (4 \times 6)$<br><br>B) $(200 \times 6) + (70 \times 6) + (4 \times 6)$ | **12.** 4.MD.1 |
| **13.** 4.NF.1 | **14.** 4.OA.1 | **15.** 4.MD.5 |

# Lesson #23

1.  Which of these is a line?  Draw it in the box.

2.  The Carol Carroll's Christmas Carols TV fundraiser earned $257 in hour one, $343 in hour two, $126 in hour three, and $74 in hour four.  They have one more hour to reach their goal of $1,000.  Which equation correctly shows this?

3.  **An angle that measures less than 90° is an acute angle.**

    Draw this acute angle.

    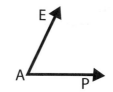

4.  Give the base-ten number: 7,000 + 400 + 60 + 5.

5.  When comparing fractions with like denominators, simply compare the numerators.  Choose the sign that makes this sentence true.  < > =

6.  3,702 − 1,965 = ?

7.  Karen typed 12 letters for her boss today.  That is 3 times as many letters as she typed on Tuesday.  Choose the best equation and use it to find out how many letters Karen typed on Tuesday.

8.  3,758 $\bigcirc$ 3,578

9.  Find all the factor pairs for 35.

10. Thorton got his dog a leash that was 72 inches long.  How many yards was the leash?

11. **Composite Numbers:  A composite number has more than two factors.**
    **12 is a composite number with 6 factors:  1, 2, 3, 4, 6, 12.**
    Is 6 a composite number?  If so, what are its factors?

12. **3 doubled is 6.  Here is a number sentence that says the same thing:**
    **3 × 2 = 6.**   Write and solve a number sentence for 9 doubled.

13. What is the length of side Q?

14. Round 4,592 to the nearest thousand.

15. Which shows the use of the distributive property for 361 × 2?

| | | |
|---|---|---|
| **1.**  4.G.1 | **2.**  4.OA.3<br><br>A) $1,000 + x = 257 + 343 + 126 + 74$<br><br>B) $257 + 343 + 126 + 74 + x = 1,000$ | **3.**  4.G.1 |
| **4.**  4.NBT.2 | **5.**  4.NF.2<br><br>$$\frac{2}{4} \bigcirc \frac{1}{4}$$ | **6.**  4.NBT.4 |
| **7.**  4.OA.2<br><br>A) $3 \times t = 12$<br><br>B) $3 \times 12 = t$ | **8.**  4.NBT.2 | **9.**  4.OA.4 |
| **10.**  4.MD.1 | **11.**  4.OA.4 | **12.**  4.OA.1 |
| **13.**  3.MD.8<br><br>4 in.<br>5 in.  perimeter: 26 cm  Q<br>5 in.<br>3 in.  3 in. | **14.**  4.NBT.3 | **15.**  4.NBT.5<br><br>A) $(300 \times 2) + (60 \times 2) + (1 \times 2)$<br><br>B) $(300 \times 2) + (60 \times 2) + (10 \times 2)$ |

# Lesson #24

1.      Which shows the use of the distributive property for 957 × 3?

2.      32 ÷ 8 = ?

3.      Is ∠CAB an acute angle or a right angle?

4.      86,470 − 38,592 = ?

5.      Stacey went off the diving board that was 60 inches high. How many feet high was the diving board?

6.      9,877 ◯ 9,788

7.      **A multiple is the product of two whole numbers. When you skip count by twos, you say the multiples of two.** List the first 5 multiples of two.

8.      Tanya received 5 times as many votes as Steve. Steve received 6 votes. How many votes did Tanya receive?

9.      The Carrot Inn attracted 153 guests on weekend one and twice that many on weekend two. About how many people stayed over the course of the two weekends, 350, 400, 450, or 500?

10.     16,775 + 9,832 = ?

11.     Draw a fraction model to show that $\frac{4}{8}$ and $\frac{3}{6}$ are equivalent.

12.     Use the protractor to draw a 60° angle. Label it ∠QWE.

13.     Write the base-ten number for eight thousand, six hundred twenty-nine.

14.     Which of these is a line segment? Draw it in the box.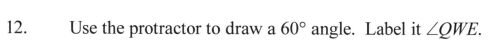

15.     Danny went into the zoo gift store with $18.32. He came out with $12.93. How much money did Danny spend in the gift shop?

| | | |
|---|---|---|
| **1.**      4.NBT.5<br><br>A) $(9{,}000 \times 3) + (50 \times 3) + (7 \times 3)$<br><br>B) $(900 \times 3) + (50 \times 3) + (7 \times 3)$ | **2.**      3.OA.7 | **3.**      4.G.1<br> |
| **4.**      4.NBT.4 | **5.**      4.MD.1 | **6.**      4.NBT.2 |
| **7.**      4.OA.4 | **8.**      4.OA.1 | **9.**      4.OA.3 |
| **10.**      4.NBT.4 | **11.**      4.NF.1 | **12.**      4.MD.6<br> |
| **13.**      4.NBT.2 | **14.**      4.G.1 | **15.**      4.MD.2 |

# Lesson #25

1.   **One hour (hr) is 60 minutes (min).**  Write 1 hr = 60 min in the box.

2.   61,388 + 92,333 = ?

3.   5,000 − 1,693 = ?

4.   Use the distributive property to multiply 184 × 5.

5.   William found the missing comic book from his collection! It cost $2.10, and he paid for it with dimes.  How many dimes did William use to buy the comic book?

6.   6,541 − 3,986 = ?

7.   9 × 5 = ?

8.   Keira watched 23 hours of TV this week.  That is 13 more hours than she watched last week.  How many hours of TV did Keira watch last week?  Choose the correct equation and solve it.

9.   Draw an acute angle.

10.  24 ÷ 8 = ?

11.  Mario Freedman read several pages a day for 2 weeks.  Here are his page-reading counts from week one: 25, 35, 75, 65, and 10.  During week two, he read the same number of pages.  About how many total pages did he read, 200, 400, or 600?  Use compatible numbers.

12.  List the first 5 multiples of 6.

13.  Draw $\overline{PT}$.

14.  Is $\angle LKJ$ acute or right?

15.  Round 46,544 to the nearest thousand.

| 1.  4.MD.1 | 2.  4.NBT.4 | 3.  4.NBT.4 |
|---|---|---|
| **4.**  4.NBT.5 | **5.**  4.MD.2 | **6.**  4.NBT.4 |
| **7.**  3.OA.7 | **8.**  4.OA.2<br><br>A)  $23 + 13 = v$<br><br>B)  $13 + v = 23$ | **9.**  4.G.1 |
| **10.**  3.OA.7 | **11.**  4.OA.3 | **12.**  4.OA.4 |
| **13.**  4.G.1 | **14.**  4.G.1 | **15.**  4.NBT.3 |

# Lesson #26

1.     $9,000 - 3,641 = ?$

2.     Choose the sign that makes this sentence true.  ($<$, $>$, $=$)

3.     One hour (hr) equals _____ minutes (min).

4.     $35,888 + 29,716 = ?$

5.     Use the distributive property to multiply $519 \times 2$.

6.     Round 86,492 to the nearest ten thousand.

7.     $30,000 = 3,000 \times$ _____

8.     Molly biked 4 times as many miles as Ollie. Ollie biked 8 miles. How many miles did Molly bike?

9.     Doris Knight baked 102 pies each during weeks 1, 2, and 3. During week 4, she baked 120. Customers bought 300 total pies. About how many pies did <u>not</u> sell, 100 or 200?

10.    Draw a right angle. How many degrees are in a right angle?

11.    Write 3,069 using words.

12.    Jerry counted 18 deer on his nature walk. That is 9 times as many as he counted on his walk last Tuesday. Choose the best equation and use it to find out how many deer Jerry saw on Tuesday.

13.    Write 81,322 in expanded form.

14.    Is 25 prime or composite? Explain.

15.    Is $\angle TLB$ acute or right?

| | | |
|---|---|---|
| **1.**    4.NBT.4 | **2.**    4.NF.2 $$\frac{5}{10} \bigcirc \frac{9}{10}$$ | **3.**    4.MD.1 |
| **4.**    4.NBT.4 | **5.**    4.NBT.5 | **6.**    4.NBT.3 |
| **7.**    4.NBT.1 | **8.**    4.OA.1 | **9.**    4.OA.3 |
| **10.**    4.G.1 | **11.**    4.NBT.2 | **12.**    4.OA.2 <br> A) $18 \times 9 = d$ <br><br> B) $9 \times d = 18$ |
| **13.**    4.NBT.2 | **14.**    4.OA.4 | **15.**    4.G.1 <br> |

# Lesson #27

1. Here's an example of the distributive property used to multiply $1,452 \times 5$.

   • Multiply 5 by all the values in 1,452 $(1,000 + 400 + 50 + 2)$.
   • $(1,000 \times 5) + (400 \times 5) + (50 \times 5) + (2 \times 5) = 5,000 + 2,000 + 250 + 10 = 7,260$.

   Use the distributive property to multiply $1,273 \times 3$.

2. $3,375 + 4,869 = ?$

3. Is $\angle EMH$ acute, right, or obtuse?

4. Write 1,923 using words.

5. Is 16 prime or composite? Explain.

6. Round 4,206 to the nearest hundred.

7. $9,385 - 3,218 = ?$

8. Draw a fraction model to show that $\frac{1}{2}$ and $\frac{5}{10}$ are equivalent.

9. If 1 hr = 60 min, then 2 hr = _____.

10. An angle that measures less than 90 degrees is an acute angle. Draw an acute angle.

11. After trick-or-treating, Mackenzie lined up her candy end to end. It measured 7 feet long. If she ate a foot of candy that night, how many inches were left?

12. Fill in the sign to make this sentence true.     21,312 ◯ 21,693

13. Sasha counted 64 butterflies at the Botanical Gardens on Monday. That is 8 times as many as she counted on Saturday. Choose the best equation and use it to find out how many butterflies Sasha counted on Saturday.

14. Write the base-ten number for $50,000 + 4,000 + 200 + 90 + 9$.

15. Ceilia donated twice as many cans of food to the food drive than her brother. He gave 9 cans. How many cans of food did Ceilia donate?

| | | |
|---|---|---|
| **1.**      4.NBT.5 | **2.**      4.NBT.4 | **3.**      4.G.1 |
| **4.**      4.NBT.2 | **5.**      4.OA.4 | **6.**      4.NBT.3 |
| **7.**      4.NBT.4 | **8.**      4.NF.1 | **9.**      4.MD.1 |
| **10.**      4.G.1 | **11.**      4.MD.2 | **12.**      4.NBT.2 |
| **13.**      4.OA.2 <br><br> A) $8 \times 64 = b$ <br><br> B) $8 \times b = 64$ | **14.**      4.NBT.2 | **15.**      4.OA.1 |

# Lesson #28

1. Fill in the sign that makes this number sentence true.    712,585 $\bigcirc$ 712,858
   The numbers are the same until the _____ place.

2. The bird flew 1 yard before landing in the tree.  How many feet did the bird fly?

3. Write and solve a number sentence for *7 tripled*.

4. $6,372 + 4,768 = ?$

5. Is the measure of $\angle TOY$ most likely to be 40°, 90°, or 120°?

6. Round 38,741 to the nearest thousand.

7. Here's an example of the distributive property used to multiply $1,452 \times 3$.

    •$(1,000 \times 3) + (400 \times 3) + (50 \times 3) + (2 \times 3) = 3,000 + 1,200 + 150 + 6 = 4,356$.

    Use the distributive property to multiply $1,564 \times 4$.

8. $4 \times 5 = ?$

9. For four years, Maryann collected baseball cards.  In year A, she collected 205.
   In year B, she collected 198.  In year C, she collected 302.  At the end of year
   D, she had collected about 900 cards altogether.  About how many cards did she
   collect in year D, 100, 200, or 300?

10. List the first 5 multiples of 9.

11. Pete sawed a 6-foot tree into 4 equal sections for firewood.  How many
    inches long was each section?

12. $48 \div 6 = ?$

13. Choose the sign that makes this sentence true.

14. $65,210 - 38,463 = ?$

15. $\angle RBT$ is a right angle.  Draw it.

| | | |
|---|---|---|
| **1.**  4.NBT.2 <br><br> A) ones <br> B) tens <br> C) hundreds <br> D) thousands | **2.**  4.MD.1 | **3.**  4.OA.1 |
| **4.**  4.NBT.4 | **5.**  4.MD.6 <br><br> | **6.**  4.NBT.3 |
| **7.**  4.NBT.5 | **8.**  3.OA.7 | **9.**  4.OA.3 |
| **10.**  4.OA.4 | **11.**  4.MD.2 | **12.**  3.OA.7 |
| **13.**  4.NF.2 <br><br> $\dfrac{8}{12} \bigcirc \dfrac{6}{12}$ | **14.**  4.NBT.4 | **15.**  4.G.1 |

# Lesson #29

1.  The king's general hired 212 knights in year A, 116 in year B, 281 in year C, and 277 in year D.  By the end of year D, 100 knights had quit.  About how many knights did he have at the end of year D, 700, 800, or 900?

2.  Is 31 prime or composite?  Explain.

3.  Lilly picked 35 flowers on Wednesday.  That is 5 times as many as she picked on Sunday.  Choose the best equation and use it to find out how many flowers she picked on Sunday.

4.  $4,000 - 1,639 = ?$

5.  Is the measure of $\angle CAT$ most likely to be 30°, 60°, or 100°?

6.  Fill in the sign that makes this number sentence true.   41,301 $\bigcirc$ 41,310
    In which place value does the value change?

7.  Draw a fraction model to show that $\frac{1}{4}$ and $\frac{2}{8}$ are equivalent.

8.  Nikko had $25.00.  He wanted to buy soccer supplies.  He spent $10.34 on shin guards, $7.51 on cones, and $1.43 on a water bottle.  How much money did Nikko have left?

9.  Write and solve a number sentence for 7 doubled.

10. Draw an acute angle.

11. The turkey had to roast for 4 hours.  How many minutes is that?

12. Round 61,987 to the nearest ten thousand.

13. $272,814 + 561,554 = ?$

14. Find the area.

15. **Angles are formed wherever two rays share a common endpoint.**  Draw the angle that is formed where $\overrightarrow{MN}$ and $\overrightarrow{MO}$ share a common endpoint.

| 1. 4.OA.3 | 2. 4.OA.4 | 3. 4.OA.2 <br> A) $35 \times 5 = f$ <br> B) $5 \times f = 35$ |
|---|---|---|
| 4. 4.NBT.4 | 5. 4.MD.6 <br> | 6. 4.NBT.2 |
| 7. 4.NF.1 | 8. 4.MD.2 | 9. 4.OA.1 |
| 10. 4.G.1 | 11. 4.MD.1 | 12. 4.NBT.3 |
| 13. 4.NBT.4 | 14. 3.MD.7 <br> <br> 8 ft <br> 8 ft | 15. 4.MD.5 |

# Lesson #30

1. Use the distributive property to multiply 3,421 × 5.
   Multiply 5 by all the values in 3,421 (3,000 + 400 + 20 + 1).

2. 9,246 + 12,389 = ?

3. Simon jumped 1 foot. How many inches did he jump?

4. Is the measure of ∠*BUG* most likely to be 20°, 50°, or 80°?

5. Is 19 prime or composite? Explain.

6. Patrick found 83 acorns on his nature hike. That is 15 more than Tommy found.
   How many acorns did Tommy find? Choose the correct equation and solve it.

7. 200,000 = 20,000 × \_\_\_\_\_

8. Fill in the sign that makes this number sentence true.    421,678 ◯ 420,678
   The numbers are the same until the _____ place.

9. Round 813 to the nearest hundred.

10. Kazuko Horne loves drawing unicorns. She drew 227 unicorns in year A, 198
    in year B, and 319 in year C. By the end of year D, she has a total of 1,000
    unicorn pictures. If your goal is to find the number drawn in year D, which
    equation represents the problem?

11. 500 − 275 = ?

12. Which of these is a ray? Draw it.

13. Choose the sign that makes this sentence true.    < > =

14. **An angle that measures greater than 90 degrees is an obtuse angle.**
    Draw an obtuse angle.

15. Write and solve a number sentence for 4 doubled.

| | | |
|---|---|---|
| **1.**   4.NBT.5 | **2.**   4.NBT.4 | **3.**   4.MD.1 |
| **4.**   4.MD.6 | **5.**   4.OA.4 | **6.**   4.OA.2 <br><br> A) $83 + 15 = a$ <br><br> B) $15 + a = 83$ |
| **7.**   4.NBT.1 | **8.**   4.NBT.2 <br><br> A) ones <br> B) tens <br> C) hundreds <br> D) thousands | **9.**   4.NBT.3 |
| **10.**   4.OA.3 <br><br> A) $1,000 - 227 - 198 - 319 = y$ <br><br> B) $227 + 198 + 319 - y = 1,000$ | **11.**   4.NBT.4 | **12.**   4.G.1 |
| **13.**   4.NF.2 <br><br> $\dfrac{4}{6}$ ◯ $\dfrac{5}{6}$ | **14.**   4.G.1 | **15.**   4.OA.1 |

# Lesson #31

1.      5,902 + 4,878 = ?

2.      Is the measure of ∠*SAY* most likely to be 45°, 90°, or 105°?

3.      Use the distributive property to multiply 2,546 × 2.
        Multiply 2 by all the values in 2,546.  Show the product.

4.      Fill in the sign that makes this number sentence true.   57,459 ◯ 57,458
        The numbers are the same until the _____ place.

5.      187,343 + 652,444 = ?

6.      If ∠*DEF* is a right angle, what is the measure of *n* ?

7.      Write and solve a number sentence for 6 doubled.

8.      Anna Beth worked on her book project for an hour and 15 minutes on Monday,
        25 minutes on Wednesday, and 10 minutes on Friday.  What was the total
        number of minutes Anna Beth spent on her book project?

9.      Kimberly used 12 different colors of paint in her picture.  That is 2 times as
        many as Kelly used.  Choose the best equation and use it to find out how many
        colors Kelly used in her painting.

10.     Is 47 prime or composite?  Explain.

11.     Draw an acute angle.

12.     5,202 − 2,863 = ?

13.     Round 3,640 to the nearest hundred.

14.     _____ are measured in degrees.

15.     It took the Nobles 420 minutes to drive to their grandparents' house.
        How many hours did the Nobles drive?

| 1.    4.NBT.4 | 2.    4.MD.6 | 3.    4.NBT.5 |
|---|---|---|
|  | |  |
| 4.    4.NBT.2 <br><br> A) ones <br> B) tens <br> C) hundreds <br> D) thousands | 5.    4.NBT.4 | 6.    4.MD.7 <br> |
| 7.    4.OA.1 | 8.    4.MD.2 | 9.    4.OA.2 <br><br> A) $2 \times c = 12$ <br><br> B) $12 \times 2 = c$ |
| 10.    4.OA.4 | 11.    4.G.1 | 12.    4.NBT.4 |
| 13.    4.NBT.3 | 14.    4.MD.5 | 15.    4.MD.1 |

# Lesson #32

1.      $364{,}265 + 276{,}855 = ?$

2.      Is $\angle DLM$ acute, right, or obtuse?

3.      Write and solve a number sentence for 8 doubled.

4.      Fill in the numerator to show an equivalent fraction.

5.      Round 7,912 to the nearest thousand.

6.      Use the distributive property to multiply $5{,}271 \times 6$.
           Multiply 6 by all the values in 5,271.  Show the product.

7.      Hazel loves to watch TV.  Today she watched a movie that was 2 hours long, a science program that was 20 minutes long, and a comedy that was 45 minutes long.  Give the total number of minutes that Hazel spent watching TV today.

8.      Is 60 prime or composite?  Explain.

9.      $700 - 568 = ?$

10.     Timmy's mom did 12 loads of laundry this week.
         That is 5 more loads than she did last week.
         How many loads of laundry did Timmy's mom do
         last week?  Choose the correct equation and solve it.

11.     If a half-hour is 30 minutes, a whole hour is _____ minutes.

12.     Angles are formed wherever two _____ share a common endpoint.

13.     Franklin's Foods supplied 87 school cafeterias with food in year A.  In year B, 113 new schools started using the company.  In year C, Franklin's Foods lost 27 schools as customers.  About how many school cafeterias did Franklin's Foods provide food to, 150, 175, or 200?

14.     Draw an obtuse angle.

15.     **A straight angle measures 180°.**  If $\angle ABC$ is a straight angle, what is the measure of $y$?

| 1. 4.NBT.4 | 2. 4.G.1 | 3. 4.OA.1 |
|---|---|---|

2.

| 4. 4.NF.1 | 5. 4.NBT.3 | 6. 4.NBT.5 |
|---|---|---|

4.
$$\frac{1}{3} = \frac{\Box}{6}$$

| 7. 4.MD.2 | 8. 4.OA.4 | 9. 4.NBT.4 |
|---|---|---|

| 10. 4.OA.2 | 11. 4.MD.1 | 12. 4.MD.5 |
|---|---|---|

10.
A) $12 + 5 = x$

B) $x + 5 = 12$

| 13. 4.OA.3 | 14. 4.G.1 | 15. 4.MD.7 |
|---|---|---|

15.

# Lesson #33

1. Draw a right angle formed from $\overrightarrow{MN}$ and $\overrightarrow{MO}$. Both rays have endpoint M in common.

2. 120 kids played in the soccer tournament in year A. In year B, the tournament had twice as many kids as in year A. In year C, there were 60 more than B. How many kids played in year C?

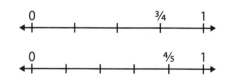

3. $70,000 = \underline{\hspace{1cm}} \times 10$

4. $47,802 - 39,986 = ?$

5. Each week, Chloe takes 2 hours of ballet. She takes 40 minutes of tap, 30 minutes of jazz, and 1 hour of lyrical. How many minutes does Chloe spend on dance lessons each week?

6. Use the distributive property to multiply $4,561 \times 7$.
   Multiply 7 by all the values in 4,561. Show the product.

7. Round 3,014 to the nearest thousand.

8. Is the measure of $\angle COW$ most likely to be 120°, 150°, or 170°?

9. Is 10 prime or composite? Explain.

10. Choose the sign that makes the sentence true. Find the fractions on each number line. The fraction that is farthest to the right is greater.

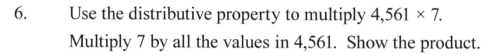

11. **Two lines are parallel if they never intersect and are always the same distance apart.** Draw $\overleftrightarrow{QR}$ parallel to $\overleftrightarrow{ST}$ in the box.

12. Tyrone sleeps on the top of his loft bed. The bed is 6 feet off the ground. How many yards is his bed off the ground?

13. Fill in the sign that makes this number sentence true.    $98,546 \bigcirc 97,546$
    The numbers are the same until the $\underline{\hspace{2cm}}$ place.

14. Write and solve a number sentence for 2 doubled.

15. $19 \div 4 = ?$

| 1.      4.G.1 | 2.      4.OA.3 | 3.      4.NBT.1 |
|---|---|---|
| 4.      4.NBT.4 | 5.      4.MD.2 | 6.      4.NBT.5 |
| 7.      4.NBT.3 | 8.      4.MD.6 | 9.      4.OA.4 |
| 10.      4.NF.2 $$\frac{3}{4} \bigcirc \frac{4}{5}$$ | 11.      4.G.1 | 12.      4.MD.1 |
| 13.      4.NBT.2 <br><br> A) ones <br> B) tens <br> C) hundreds <br> D) thousands | 14.      4.OA.1 | 15.      3.OA.7 |

# Lesson #34

1. Write and solve a number sentence for 10 doubled.

2. Use the distributive property to multiply 3,522 × 8.
   Multiply 8 by all the values in 3,522.

3. List the first 5 multiples of 5.

4. If ∠MNO is a straight angle, what is the measure of f?

5. Fill in the sign that makes this number sentence true.   45,455 ◯ 45,544
   The numbers are the same until the _____ place.

6. The bird flew 1 yard before landing in the tree.  How many inches did the bird
   fly?

7. Lee's grandmother gave him $18.20 to split evenly with his sister.  How much
   money did each child get?

8. Round 33,222 to the nearest ten thousand.

9. Is ∠JHV acute, right, or obtuse?

10. Teagan ate 5 lollipops this week.  That was 2 more than her brother, Connor, ate.
    How many lollipops did Connor eat?  Choose the correct equation and solve it.

11. Write another equivalent fraction for $\frac{2}{3}$.

12. 8,492 + 7,588 = ?

13. 6,000 = _____ × 10

14. Draw parallel horizontal lines.

15. 6,000 − 986 = ?

| 1.       4.OA.1 | 2.       4.NBT.5 | 3.       4.OA.4 |
|---|---|---|

**4.**       4.MD.7

**5.**       4.NBT.2

A)  ones

B)  tens

C)  hundreds

D)  thousands

**6.**       4.MD.1

| 7.       4.MD.2 | 8.       4.NBT.3 | 9.       4.G.1 |
|---|---|---|

**10.**       4.OA.2

A) $2 + p = 5$

B) $5 + 2 = p$

**11.**       4.NF.1

$$\frac{2}{3} = \frac{4}{6} = \frac{\square}{\square}$$

**12.**       4.NBT.4

| 13.       4.NBT.1 | 14.       4.G.1 | 15.       4.NBT.4 |
|---|---|---|

# Lesson #35

1.      List the first 5 multiples of 2.

2.      Use the distributive property to multiply $187 \times 4$.

3.      If $\angle P$ is a right angle, what is the measure of $q$?

4.      $234{,}885 + 592{,}313 = ?$

5.      It took Junior 46 minutes to mow his front yard. It took him 1 hour and
        17 minutes to mow the backyard. How many more minutes did it take
        Junior to mow the backyard than the front yard?

6.      $623 - 179 = ?$

7.      Is $\angle PLK$ acute, right, or obtuse?

8.      Write and solve a number sentence for *5 tripled*.

9.      Write 56,921 in expanded form. $50{,}000 + \underline{\quad\quad} + \underline{\quad\quad} + 20 + \underline{\quad\quad}$

10.     $6{,}345 \bigcirc 6{,}435$

11.     _____ are formed wherever two rays share a common endpoint.

12.     Write 3,096 using words.

13.     Choose the sign that makes the sentence true.

14.     An angle greater than 90° is called a(n) _____ angle.

15.     Darius wants to finish a five-part race in 500 seconds
        or less. His times for the first four parts are 93 seconds,
        102 seconds, 107 seconds, and 98 seconds. Write an equation
        to show the time Darius must achieve to finish the race in 500 seconds.
        Use $x$ to represent the unknown time.

| | | |
|---|---|---|
| **1.**    4.OA.4 | **2.**    4.NBT.5 | **3.**    4.MD.7 |
| **4.**    4.NBT.4 | **5.**    4.MD.2 | **6.**    4.NBT.4 |
| **7.**    4.G.1 | **8.**    4.OA.1 | **9.**    4.NBT.2 |
| **10.**    4.NBT.2 | **11.**    4.MD.5 | **12.**    4.NBT.2 |
| **13.**    4.NF.2 $$\frac{11}{12} \bigcirc \frac{9}{12}$$ | **14.**    4.G.1 | **15.**    4.OA.3 |

# Lesson #36

1. $57 \div 9 = ?$

2. Draw an acute angle formed from $\overrightarrow{WV}$ and $\overrightarrow{WZ}$.

3. Rocco swam 24 inches farther than Carmi. How many feet farther did Rocco swim?

4. List the first 5 multiples of 10.

5. Marcella practiced the piano for 2 hours and 26 minutes today. Yesterday she practiced for 1 hour and 5 minutes. How many more minutes did Marcella practice today than yesterday?

6. Dave watched 18 hours of TV this week. That is 10 more hours than he watched last week. How many hours of TV did Dave watch last week? Choose the correct equation and solve it.

7. Is the measure of $\angle TAG$ most likely to be 135°, 90°, or 45°?

8. $83,479 + 69,823 = ?$

9. Round 27,414 to the nearest thousand.

10. If $\angle XYZ$ is a straight angle, what is the measure of $h$?

11. $700 - 196 = ?$

12. Use the distributive property to multiply $2,124 \times 9$. Multiply 9 by all the values in 2,124.

13. Fill in the denominator to show an equivalent fraction.

14. Write and solve a number sentence for *8 tripled*.

15. Fill in the sign that makes this number sentence true.  468,275 $\bigcirc$ 468,279
The numbers are the same until the _____ place.

| 1.        3.OA.7 | 2.        4.G.1 | 3.        4.MD.1 |
|---|---|---|
| 4.        4.OA.4 | 5.        4.MD.2 | 6.        4.OA.2<br><br>A) $18 + 10 = v$<br><br>B) $10 + v = 18$ |
| 7.        4.MD.6<br> | 8.        4.NBT.4 | 9.        4.NBT.3 |
| 10.       4.MD.7<br> | 11.       4.NBT.4 | 12.       4.NBT.5 |
| 13.       4.NF.1<br><br>$$\frac{1}{3} = \frac{2}{\square}$$ | 14.       4.OA.1 | 15.       4.NBT.2 |

# Lesson #37

1. **One meter (m) is 100 centimeters (cm).** Write 1 m = 100 cm in the box.

2. $378,241 + 256,479 = ?$

3. Write 6,521 in expanded form.

4. $600 - 541 = ?$

5. Write and solve a number sentence for *4 tripled.*

6. List the first 5 multiples of 3.

7. Is $\angle BDT$ acute, right, or obtuse?

8. Choose the sign that makes this sentence true. $< \ > \ =$

9. Round 42,375 to the nearest thousand.

10. Sam built a $3\frac{1}{2}$ foot long bridge over the creek. How many inches long was the bridge?

11. $800,000 = \underline{\hspace{1cm}} \times 10$

12. Which lines are parallel?     A)    B)    C)    D)

13. A trawler catches 147 scallops during hour A, 134 during hour B, 103 during hour C, and 66 during hour D. If the trawler catches the same number the next day, how many will it have caught in total?

14. If $\angle TSR$ is a right angle, what is the measure of *a*?

15. $62 \times 5 = ?$

| | | |
|---|---|---|
| **1.** 4.MD.1 | **2.** 4.NBT.4 | **3.** 4.NBT.2 |
| **4.** 4.NBT.4 | **5.** 4.OA.1 | **6.** 4.OA.4 |
| **7.** 4.G.1 | **8.** 4.NF.2 $$\frac{51}{100} \bigcirc \frac{50}{100}$$ | **9.** 4.NBT.3 |
| **10.** 4.MD.2 | **11.** 4.NBT.1 | **12.** 4.G.1 |
| **13.** 4.OA.3 | **14.** 4.MD.7 | **15.** 4.NBT.5 |

# Lesson #38

1. Write the base-ten number for $3,000 + 800 + 50 + 7$.

2. Write another equivalent fraction for $\frac{1}{4}$.

3. Round 3,576 to the nearest hundred.

4. The gumball machine only takes quarters. Paige put in $1.75. How many quarters was that?

5. One meter (m) equals _____ centimeters (cm).

6. Fill in the sign that makes this number sentence true.     $23,281 \bigcirc 21,281$
   The numbers are the same until the _____ place.

7. Is the measure of $\angle SUP$ most likely to be 15°, 45°, or 75°?

8. Elisa Turtell spent $27 at the mall on day one, $55 on day 2, and $73 on day three. The next week, she spent three times that much. About how much did she spend <u>in total</u>, $450, $600, or $750?

9. $4,267 + 5,985 = ?$

10. List the first 5 multiples of 4.

11. Write and solve a number sentence for *9 tripled*.

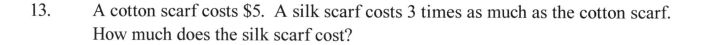

12. Describe the pattern.      1, 3, 5, 7, 9

13. A cotton scarf costs $5. A silk scarf costs 3 times as much as the cotton scarf. How much does the silk scarf cost?

14. $800 - 365 = ?$

15. If $\angle DEF$ is a straight angle, what is the measure of $z$?

| | | |
|---|---|---|
| **1.**    4.NBT.2 | **2.**    4.NF.1 <br><br> $$\dfrac{1}{4} = \dfrac{2}{8} = \dfrac{\boxed{\phantom{0}}}{\boxed{\phantom{0}}}$$ | **3.**    4.NBT.3 |
| **4.**    4.MD.2 | **5.**    4.MD.1 | **6.**    4.NBT.2 |
| **7.**    4.MD.6 <br><br> | **8.**    4.OA.3 | **9.**    4.NBT.4 |
| **10.**    4.OA.4 | **11.**    4.OA.1 | **12.**    4.OA.5 |
| **13.**    4.OA.2 <br><br><table><tr><td>Cotton</td><td>\$5</td><td>\$5</td><td>\$5</td></tr><tr><td>Silk</td><td colspan="3">\$ ?</td></tr></table><br> $\$5 \times 3 =$ _____ | **14.**    4.NBT.4 | **15.**    4.MD.7 <br><br> |

# Lesson #39

1.    357 + 494 = ?

2.    5,000 − 1,379 = ?

3.    Choose the sign that makes this sentence true.

4.    Toya walked 12 yards to her car on Monday and 8 yards to her car on Tuesday. How many yards did Toya walk to her car over those two days?  How many feet did she walk?

5.    Round 465 to the nearest hundred.

6.    Find the measure of $\angle PQR$.

7.    If 1 m = 100 cm, then 2 m = _____ cm.

8.    Use the distributive property to multiply 4,309 × 4.  Find the product.

9.    Is 44 prime or composite?  Explain.

10.   If $\angle AGS$ is a straight angle, what is the measure of $t$?

11.   Fill in the sign that makes this number sentence true.      82,442 ◯ 82,244
      The numbers are the same until the _____ place.

12.   Describe the pattern.      2, 7, 12, 17, 22

13.   **Two lines are perpendicular if they intersect and form a right angle (90°).  Draw a pair of perpendicular lines in the box.**

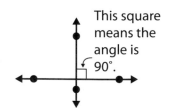

This square means the angle is 90°.

14.   44 ÷ 6 = ?

15.   The price for a hot dog at the stadium is $2.  A hamburger costs 4 times as much as a hot dog.  How much does a hamburger cost?

| 1.   4.NBT.4 | 2.   4.NBT.4 | 3.   4.NF.2 |
|---|---|---|
| | | $$\dfrac{5}{10} \bigcirc \dfrac{7}{10}$$ |

| 4.   4.MD.2 | 5.   4.NBT.3 | 6.   4.MD.6 |
|---|---|---|
| | | |

| 7.   4.MD.1 | 8.   4.NBT.5 | 9.   4.OA.4 |
|---|---|---|
| | | |

| 10.   4.MD.7 | 11.   4.NBT.2 | 12.   4.OA.5 |
|---|---|---|
| | | |

| 13.   4.G.1 | 14.   3.OA.7 | 15.   4.OA.2 |
|---|---|---|
| | | |

**15.** table:

| Hamburger | ? | | | |
|---|---|---|---|---|
| Hot Dog | $2 | $2 | $2 | $2 |

$2 × 4 = _____

# Lesson #40

1.      The distance between Gigi's house and school is 1 mile.  The distance between Susan's house and school is 6 times as far.  How far is it from Susan's house to school?

2.      Fill in the sign that makes this number sentence true.      512,234 ◯ 512,284
         The numbers are the same until the _____ place.

3.      Find all the factor pairs for 21.

4.      Round 56,419 to the nearest ten thousand.

5.      7,000 − 3,433 = ?

6.      Describe the pattern.         1, 5, 9, 13, 17

7.      40,000 = _____ × 10

8.      42 ÷ 7 = ?

9.      Draw $\overline{LM}$ .

10.     Find the measure of ∠CDE.

11.     Carla is 1 meter tall.  How many centimeters tall is she?

12.     Maggie spent 120 minutes reading at the library.  How many hours did Maggie spend reading?

13.     If ∠EFG is a right angle, what is the measure of k?

14.     Fill in the numerator to show an equivalent fraction.

15.     8,459 + 7,666 = ?

| 1.     4.OA.2 | 2.     4.NBT.2 | 3.     4.OA.4 |
|---|---|---|
|  $1 \times 6 = $ _____ | | |

| 4.     4.NBT.3 | 5.     4.NBT.4 | 6.     4.OA.5 |
|---|---|---|
| | | |

| 7.     4.NBT.1 | 8.     3.OA.7 | 9.     4.G.1 |
|---|---|---|
| | | |

| 10.     4.MD.6 | 11.     4.MD.1 | 12.     4.MD.2 |
|---|---|---|
| 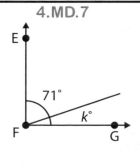 | | |

| 13.     4.MD.7 | 14.     4.NF.1 | 15.     4.NBT.4 |
|---|---|---|
| | $\dfrac{2}{4} = \dfrac{\Box}{8}$ | |

# Lesson #41

1.      Use the distributive property to multiply 6,355 × 6.  Show the product.

2.      120 ÷ 6 = ?

3.      Ralph did 56 sit ups on Friday.  That is 7 times as many as he did on Monday.
        Choose the best equation and use it to find out how many sit ups Ralph did on
        Monday.

4.      Is 72 prime or composite?  Explain.

5.      Describe the pattern.        2, 4, 6, 8, 10

6.      **One kilometer (km) is 1,000 meters (m).**  Write 1 km = 1,000 m in the box.

7.      Fill in the sign that makes this number sentence true.        61,554 ◯ 61,555
        The numbers are the same until the _____ place.

8.      Angles are formed wherever two rays share a common _____.

9.      Write 7,461 in expanded form.

10.     If ∠QRS is a straight angle, what is the measure of $v$?

11.     1,000 = _____ × 10

12.     Choose the sign that makes this sentence true.

13.     Is ∠QRV acute, right, or obtuse?

14.     6,554 + 3,862 = ?

15.     Sandy collected 8 times as many stamps from France as she collected from Italy.
        She collected 4 stamps from Italy.  How many did she collect from France?

| 1.      4.NBT.5 | 2.      4.NBT.6 | 3.      4.OA.2 |
|---|---|---|
| | | A) $7 \times s = 56$<br><br>B) $7 \times 56 = s$ |
| 4.      4.OA.4 | 5.      4.OA.5 | 6.      4.MD.1 |
| | | |
| 7.      4.NBT.2 | 8.      4.MD.5 | 9.      4.NBT.2 |
| | | |
| 10.      4.MD.7 | 11.      4.NBT.1 | 12.      4.NF.2 |
| | | $\dfrac{6}{8}\ \bigcirc\ \dfrac{5}{8}$ |
| 13.      4.G.1 | 14.      4.NBT.4 | 15.      4.OA.1 |
| | | |

# Lesson #42

1.  Round 36,435 to the nearest thousand.

2.  $3{,}788 + 9{,}862 = ?$

3.  Is the measure of $\angle DOT$ most likely to be 30°, 60°, or 80°?

4.  List the first 5 multiples of 7.

5.  Fill in the sign that makes this number sentence true.    28,162 $\bigcirc$ 28,132
    The numbers are the same until the _____ place.

6.  One kilometer (km) equals _____ meters (m).

7.  Describe the pattern.      3, 5, 7, 9, 11

    Are the numbers always even, always odd, or do they alternate?

8.  Darlene picks 125 tomatoes on day one, 187 on day two, and 115 on day three. Over the next three days, she picks almost the exact same number as on the first three.  Did she pick more or less than 800 tomatoes?

9.  Complete the matrix model to find the product.  $57 \times 48 = ?$
    See the *Help Pages* for an example.

10. Write another equivalent fraction for $\dfrac{3}{5}$.

11. Write and solve a number sentence for
    five times as many as 7.

12. If $\angle J$ is a right angle, what is the measure of $k$?

13. Draw perpendicular lines.

14. $360 \div 4 = ?$

15. $703 - 566 = ?$

| 1. 4.NBT.3 | 2. 4.NBT.4 | 3. 4.MD.6 |
|---|---|---|

| 4. 4.OA.4 | 5. 4.NBT.2 | 6. 4.MD.1 |
|---|---|---|

A) ones

B) tens

C) hundreds

D) thousands

| 7. 4.OA.5 | 8. 4.OA.3 | 9. 4.NBT.5 |
|---|---|---|

| 10. 4.NF.1 | 11. 4.OA.1 | 12. 4.MD.7 |
|---|---|---|

$$\frac{3}{5} = \frac{6}{10} = \frac{\square}{\square}$$

| 13. 4.G.1 | 14. 4.NBT.6 | 15. 4.NBT.4 |
|---|---|---|

# Lesson #43

1.  Find all the factor pairs for 33.

2.  The daylilies in Mrs. Smith's garden grew 36 inches tall. How many feet tall was each daylily?

3.  Write 32,413 in expanded form.

4.  $9,248 + 3,666 = ?$

5.  If $\angle T$ is a right angle, what is the measure of $x$?

6.  The bakery sold 6 times as many chocolate chip cookies as peanut butter cookies. They sold 7 peanut butter cookies. How many chocolate chip cookies did the bakery sell?

7.  Marina sees 124 fish on Monday, 55 on Tuesday, 76 on Wednesday, and 145 on Thursday. The next week, she sees half as many fish. How many total fish does Marina see?

8.  When comparing fractions with like denominators, simply compare the numerators. Choose the sign that makes this sentence true.

9.  Round 56,322 to the nearest thousand.

10. Use the distributive property to multiply $8,021 \times 8$. Find the product.

11. $48 \times 31 = ?$ Complete the matrix model to find the product.
    For an example, use the matrix model in the *Help Pages*.

12. $503 - 279 = ?$

13. Find the measure of $\angle LMN$.

14. $180 \div 6 = ?$

15. A daisy is 3 feet tall. A sunflower is 2 times as tall. How tall is the sunflower?

| | | |
|---|---|---|
| **1.**  4.OA.4 | **2.**  4.MD.2 | **3.**  4.NBT.2 |
| **4.**  4.NBT.4 | **5.**  4.MD.7 | **6.**  4.OA.1 |
| **7.**  4.OA.3 | **8.**  4.NF.2 $$\frac{8}{10} \bigcirc \frac{9}{10}$$ | **9.**  4.NBT.3 |
| **10.**  4.NBT.5 | **11.**  4.NBT.5 | **12.**  4.NBT.4 |
| **13.**  4.MD.6 | **14.**  4.NBT.6 | **15.**  4.OA.2  $3 \times 2 =$ _____ |

# Lesson #44

1.    Describe the pattern.   1, 4, 7, 10, 13

2.    $240 \div 6 = ?$

3.    If 1 km = 1,000 m, then 2 km = _____ m.

4.    Which lines are perpendicular?

5.    Fill in the denominator to show an equivalent fraction.

6.    If $\angle NOP$ is a straight angle, what is the measure of $s$?

7.    Carrie catches 75 fish a day for five days.  The next week, she catches 25 fish a
      day for five days.  How many fish does she catch in all?

8.    Write the base-ten number for
      $3,000 + 400 + 60 + 9$.

9.    $6,000 - 2,471 = ?$

10.   $52 \times 47 = ?$  Complete the matrix
      model to find the product.

11.   Is 13 prime or composite?  Explain.

12.   Find the perimeter of the rectangle.  Label the answer.

13.   $938 + 486 = ?$

14.   Fill in the sign that makes this number sentence true.    344,723 ◯ 244,723
      The numbers are the same until the _____ place.

15.   Mina grew 3 times as many centimeters as her older brother.  He grew 4
      centimeters.  How many centimeters did Mina grow?

| | | |
|---|---|---|
| **1.**      4.OA.5 | **2.**      4.NBT.6 | **3.**      4.MD.1 |
| **4.**      4.G.1 | **5.**      4.NF.1 $$\frac{1}{5} = \frac{2}{\square}$$ | **6.**      4.MD.7 |
| **7.**      4.OA.3 | **8.**      4.NBT.2 | **9.**      4.NBT.4 |
| **10.**      4.NBT.5 | **11.**      4.OA.4 | **12.**      4.MD.3 |
| **13.**      4.NBT.4 | **14.**      4.NBT.2 | **15.**      4.OA.1 |

# Lesson #45

1. $78 \times 23 = ?$ Complete the matrix model to find the product.

2. Is the measure of $\angle FOP$ most likely to be 10°, 30°, or 70°?

3. In Major League Baseball, there are 90 feet between the bases. How many inches is that?

4. Write 8,902 in expanded form.

5. $16,332 + 14,769 = ?$

6. List the first 5 multiples of 8.

7. $6,003 - 4,872 = ?$

8. If $\angle TUV$ is a right angle, what is the measure of $a$?

9. When comparing fractions with like denominators, simply compare the numerators. Fill in the sign that makes this sentence true.

10. $90,000 = \underline{\qquad} \times 10$

11. 450 divided by 9 = ?

12. Kym walked 3 kilometers in one hour. How many meters did Kym walk?

13. Use the distributive property to multiply $6,136 \times 4$. Find the product.

14. **Angles are measured in degrees.** Write the sentence in your box.

15. Anita makes money over the summer by doing odd jobs. She made $547 during 4 weeks in July. Look at the equation. Which of the following is the most reasonable estimate for $x$: $50, $200, or $350?

| | | |
|---|---|---|
| **1.** 4.NBT.5 | **2.** 4.MD.6 | **3.** 4.MD.2 |
| **4.** 4.NBT.2 | **5.** 4.NBT.4 | **6.** 4.OA.4 |
| **7.** 4.NBT.4 | **8.** 4.MD.7 | **9.** 4.NF.2 $\dfrac{3}{5} \bigcirc \dfrac{5}{5}$ |
| **10.** 4.NBT.1 | **11.** 4.NBT.6 | **12.** 4.MD.1 |
| **13.** 4.NBT.5 | **14.** 4.MD.5 | **15.** 4.OA.3 $\$110 + \$90 + \$150 + x = \$547$ |

# Lesson #46

1. $339 \div 3 = ?$

2. $300,000 = \underline{\hspace{1cm}} \times 10$

3. Use the distributive property to multiply $1,107 \times 2$. Show the product.

4. Fill in the denominator to show an equivalent fraction.

5. My dog, Lucy, jumped the fence 5 times today. That is 2 more times than she jumped yesterday. How many times did Lucy jump the fence yesterday? Choose the correct equation and solve it.

6. The "Welcome Home" banner was 18 feet long. To make it easy to carry, the banner was separated into 3 equal sections. How many inches long was each section?

7. List the first 10 multiples of 5.

8. The river overflowed its banks 7 times higher than it overflowed last month. Last month it overflowed by 3 feet. How many feet did it overflow this month?

9. The plane arrived at its destination 90 minutes late. How many hours late was the plane?

10. $700 - 241 = ?$

11. Find the measure of $\angle DEF$.

12. $5,555 + 6,826 = ?$

13. Fill in the sign that makes this number sentence true.    $28,162 \bigcirc 28,132$
The numbers are the same until the _____ place.

14. Round 42,365 to the nearest ten thousand.

15. A rectangle has two pairs of parallel sides. Fill in the missing side lengths. In your answer box, write the perimeter and label it.

| | | |
|---|---|---|
| **1.**       4.NBT.6 | **2.**       4.NBT.1 | **3.**       4.NBT.5 |
| **4.**       4.NF.1 $$\frac{1}{5} = \frac{2}{\Box}$$ | **5.**       4.OA.2 <br><br> A) $2 + f = 5$ <br><br> B) $2 + 5 = f$ | **6.**       4.MD.2 |
| **7.**       4.OA.4 | **8.**       4.OA.1 | **9.**       4.MD.1 |
| **10.**       4.NBT.4 | **11.**       4.MD.6 <br><br> | **12.**       4.NBT.4 |
| **13.**       4.NBT.2 <br><br> A) ones <br> B) tens <br> C) hundreds <br> D) thousands | **14.**       4.NBT.3 | **15.**       4.MD.3 <br><br> 5 cm <br><br> 10 cm |

# Lesson #47

1.    $4,398 + 5,047 = ?$

2.    $240 \div 6 = ?$

3.    Find the measure of $\angle JKL$.

4.    Describe the pattern.    3, 6, 9, 12, 15

5.    Fill in the sign that makes this sentence true.  Think about this: $\frac{2}{10} = \frac{1}{5}$.
      Which has more fifths, $\frac{1}{5}$ or $\frac{3}{5}$?

6.    Farmer Fay is shucking corn.  She shucks 57 ears of corn on Monday, 43 ears of
      corn on Tuesday, and 100 on Wednesday.  She needs to do double that amount
      by the end of the week to fulfill an order.  How many ears of corn must she
      shuck in total?

7.    $84 \times 13 = ?$  Complete the matrix model to find the product.

8.    **One kilogram (kg) is 1,000 grams (g).**  Write 1 kg = 1,000 g in the box.

9.    $109 - 68 = ?$

10.   If $\angle L$ is a right angle, what is the measure of $w$?

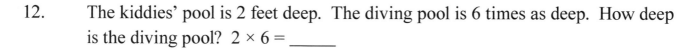

11.   List the first 10 multiples of 2.

12.   The kiddies' pool is 2 feet deep.  The diving pool is 6 times as deep.  How deep
      is the diving pool?  $2 \times 6 = $ _____

13.   Use the distributive property to multiply $3,215 \times 8$.  Find the product.

14.   Isaac can throw a ball 4 yards.  His little brother can throw a ball 2 yards.  How
      many feet is that altogether?

15.   Which lines are parallel?

| 1.      4.NBT.4 | 2.      4.NBT.6 | 3.      4.MD.6 |
|---|---|---|
| | | |

| 4.      4.OA.5 | 5.      4.NF.2 | 6.      4.OA.3 |
|---|---|---|
| | $\dfrac{2}{10} \bigcirc \dfrac{3}{5}$ | |

| 7.      4.NBT.5 | 8.      4.MD.1 | 9.      4.NBT.4 |
|---|---|---|
| | | |

| 10.      4.MD.7 | 11.      4.OA.4 | 12.      4.OA.2 |
|---|---|---|
| | | |

Table for 12:

| Diving | ? | | | | | |
|---|---|---|---|---|---|---|
| Kiddie | 2 | 2 | 2 | 2 | 2 | 2 |

| 13.      4.NBT.5 | 14.      4.MD.2 | 15.      4.G.1 |
|---|---|---|
| | | |

# Lesson #48

1. Write 3,788 in expanded form.

2. Mr. Whittaker had a class of 14 students. If he had an equal number of boys and girls, how many of each did he have? Draw a picture to help you.

3. $86 \times 90 = ?$ Complete the matrix model to find the product.

4. Grant is peeling grapes for a Halloween party. He wants to have 800 peeled grapes. He peeled 205 grapes each day for the past three days. He must peel the rest today before the party starts. About how many grapes does Grant have yet to peel, 150, 200, or 250?

5. $900 - 364 = ?$

6. $8,042 \div 2 = ?$ See *Help Pages* for place value model.

7. If $\angle OPQ$ is a straight angle, what is the measure of $b$?

8. A rectangle has two pairs of parallel sides. Fill in the missing side lengths. In your answer box, write the perimeter and label it.

9. Which lines are perpendicular?    A)    B)    C)    D)

10. Farmer Nelly picked 22 tomatoes this week. That is 11 times as many as she picked last week. Choose the best equation and use it to find out how many she picked last week.

11. Fill in the numerator to show an equivalent fraction.

12. One kilogram (kg) equals _____ grams (g).

13. Find all the factor pairs for 25.

14. Liza watched the same movie for 3 days in a row. The movie was 1 hour and 6 minutes long. How many minutes did Liza spend watching the movie?

15. Is the measure of $\angle DIG$ most likely to be 5°, 55°, or 95°?

| 1. 4.NBT.2 | 2. 3.OA.3 | 3. 4.NBT.5 |
|---|---|---|
| | | |
| 4. 4.OA.3 | 5. 4.NBT.4 | 6. 4.NBT.6 |
| | | |
| 7. 4.MD.7 | 8. 4.MD.3 | 9. 4.G.1 |
| 10. 4.OA.2 <br><br> A) $22 \times 11 = t$ <br><br> B) $11 \times t = 22$ | 11. 4.NF.1 <br><br> $\dfrac{\square}{6} = \dfrac{2}{3}$ | 12. 4.MD.1 |
| 13. 4.OA.4 | 14. 4.MD.2 | 15. 4.MD.6 |

# Lesson #49

1.    Write 6,233 using words.

2.    Use the distributive property to multiply 2,435 × 5.  Show the product.

3.    A baby humpback whale is about 1 yard long.  At 12 years old, it will be about 15 yards long.  In inches, what is the difference between the humpback's length as a baby and its length as an adult?

4.    If ∠LOB is a right angle, what is the measure of *m*?

5.    42 × 27 = ?  Complete the matrix model to find the product.

6.    A rectangle has two pairs of parallel sides.  Fill in the missing side lengths.  In your answer box, write the perimeter and label it.

7.    987 + 364 = ?

8.    Rodrigo read 8 times as many pages as Elena.  Elena read 8 pages.  How many pages did Rodrigo read?

9.    Elliette got 34 pieces of candy at the party.  That was 11 more than her brother, Easton, got.  How many pieces of candy did Easton get at the party?  Choose the correct equation and solve it.

10.    3,416 − 1,965 = ?

11.    If 1 kg = 1,000 g, then 2 kg = _____ g.

12.    Is 7 prime or composite?  Explain.

13.    Choose the sign that makes this sentence true.
Think about this: $\dfrac{8}{12} = \dfrac{4}{6}$.  Which has more sixths, $\dfrac{4}{6}$ or $\dfrac{5}{6}$?

14.    Is ∠LTY acute, right, or obtuse?

15.    Describe the pattern.  9, 11, 13, 15, 17

| 1. 4.NBT.2 | 2. 4.NBT.5 | 3. 4.MD.2 |
|---|---|---|
| 4. 4.MD.7 | 5. 4.NBT.5 | 6. 4.MD.3 |
| 7. 4.NBT.4 | 8. 4.OA.1 | 9. 4.OA.2 <br> A)  $11 + c = 34$ <br><br> B)  $1 + 34 = c$ |
| 10. 4.NBT.4 | 11. 4.MD.1 | 12. 4.OA.4 |
| 13. 4.NF.2 <br><br> $\dfrac{8}{12} \bigcirc \dfrac{5}{6}$ | 14. 4.G.1 | 15. 4.OA.5 |

# Lesson #50

1.      $6,902 - 4,766 = ?$

2.      $7,000,000 = $ _____ $\times 10$

3.      $7,986 - 3,422 = ?$

4.      Round 7,622 to the nearest hundred.

5.      Write another equivalent fraction for $\frac{3}{5}$.

6.      $37 \times 18 = ?$ Complete the matrix model to find the product.

7.      If $\angle R$ is a right angle, what is the measure of $f$?

8.      Harry's Gift Grotto ordered a thousand feet of ribbon. Each day, the store uses 200 feet of it for wrapping gifts. Let $y$ equal the unknown number of days. Which number sentence shows how many days the ribbon will last?

9.      **A two-dimensional shape has a line of symmetry if it can be folded along a line into matching parts.** Draw a triangle and show a line of symmetry.

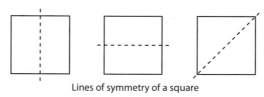

Lines of symmetry of a square

10.      The chemistry teacher's whiteboard is 400 centimeters long. How many meters long is the whiteboard?

11.      $360 \div 4 = ?$

12.      Find the measure of $\angle WXY$.

13.      List the first 10 multiples of 6.

14.      Kristin ran 5 kilometers this weekend. She ran 3 kilometers last weekend. How many meters did Kristin run in two weekends?

15.      Describe the pattern. 4, 14, 24, 34, 44     Which place value never changes?

| | | |
|---|---|---|
| **1.**     4.NBT.4 | **2.**     4.NBT.1 | **3.**     4.NBT.4 |
| **4.**     4.NBT.3 | **5.**     4.NF.1 $$\frac{3}{5} = \frac{6}{10} = \frac{\square}{\square}$$ | **6.**     4.NBT.5 |
| **7.**     4.MD.7 $f°$ $37°$ R | **8.**     4.OA.3 A) $y + y + y + y + y = 200$ B) $200 \times y = 1{,}000$ C) $y + y + y + y + y = 1{,}000$ | **9.**     4.G.3 |
| **10.**     4.MD.1 | **11.**     4.NBT.6 | **12.**     4.MD.6 |
| **13.**     4.OA.4 | **14.**     4.MD.2 | **15.**     4.OA.5 |

# Lesson #51

1. Choose the sign that makes this sentence true.

2. $6,375 + 22,489 = ?$

3. Angles are measured in _____.

4. Round 36,241 to the nearest ten thousand.

5. $8,000 - 3,566 = ?$

6. Use the distributive property to multiply $4,345 \times 2$. Find the product.

7. If 4 kg = 4,000 g, then 8 kg = _____ g.

8. Which lines are parallel?　A)　B)　C)　D)

9. Draw a line in the box. Label it CD.

10. $61 \times 74 = ?$ Complete the matrix model to find the product.

11. A rectangle has two pairs of parallel sides. Fill in the missing side lengths. In your answer box, write the perimeter and label it.

12. Write 2,598 using words.

13. Estella's mom made 54 cookies for the bake sale. That is 9 times as many as Maria's mom made. Choose the best equation and use it to find out how many cookies Maria's mom made for the bake sale.

14. If $\angle XYZ$ is a straight angle, what is the measure of $q$?

15. Sosuke makes $193 mowing lawns in week one, $102 in week two, $198 in week three, and $95 in week four. Round his earnings to the nearest 100, and use those numbers to write an equation that shows about how much he made.

| 1. 4.NF.2 | 2. 4.NBT.4 | 3. 4.MD.5 |
|---|---|---|
| $\dfrac{7}{9}$ ◯ $\dfrac{2}{3}$ | | |

| 4. 4.NBT.3 | 5. 4.NBT.4 | 6. 4.NBT.5 |
|---|---|---|
| | | |

| 7. 4.MD.1 | 8. 4.G.1 | 9. 4.G.1 |
|---|---|---|
| | | |

| 10. 4.NBT.5 | 11. 4.MD.3 | 12. 4.NBT.2 |
|---|---|---|
| | | |

| 13. 4.OA.2 | 14. 4.MD.7 | 15. 4.OA.3 |
|---|---|---|
| A) $9 \times c = 54$ <br><br> B) $9 \times 54 = c$ | | |

# Lesson #52

1. At practice Madison shot 36 hockey pucks at the goal. That is 10 more than she shot yesterday. How many hockey pucks did Madison shoot at practice yesterday? Choose the correct equation and solve it.

2. Jenni is chopping pecans for the bakery. She chops 128 pecans on Monday, 182 on Tuesday, 137 on Wednesday, and 173 on Thursday. If she chops the same number in the next four days, how many pecans will she have chopped in all?

3. Write 6,425 in expanded form.

4. Billy spent 3 hours and 34 minutes playing 18 holes of golf at Dennis Hill Golf Course. He finished the first 9 holes in half the time. How many minutes did Billy take to play the other 9 holes of golf?

5. $5,800 - 3,236 = ?$

6. $3 \times (2 \times 4) = ?$

7. Fill in the denominator to show an equivalent fraction.

8. Marla rode her horse 7 kilometers after school. How many meters did Marla ride on her horse?

9. $6,244 + 5,386 = ?$

10. A rectangle has two pairs of parallel sides. Fill in the missing side lengths. In your answer box, write the perimeter and label it.

11. If $\angle ATL$ is a right angle, what is the measure of $z$?

12. Describe the pattern. 5, 10, 15, 20, 25

13. 24 is a multiple of 1, 2, 3, _____, _____, _____, 12, and 24.

14. Is the measure of $\angle WAS$ most likely to be 30°, 70°, or 110°?

15. Draw line segment $\overline{PQ}$.

Simple Solutions©                                Common Core Mathematics 4

| 1.      4.OA.2 <br><br> A) $10 + h = 36$ <br><br> B) $10 + 36 = h$ | 2.      4.OA.3 | 3.      4.NBT.2 |
|---|---|---|
| 4.      4.MD.2 | 5.      4.NBT.4 | 6.      3.OA.5 |
| 7.      4.NF.1 <br><br> $\dfrac{2}{10} = \dfrac{20}{\square}$ | 8.      4.MD.1 | 9.      4.NBT.4 |
| 10.      4.MD.3 <br><br> 5 cm, 8 cm rectangle ____ | 11.      4.MD.7 <br> angle A, z°, 34°, T, L | 12.      4.OA.5 |
| 13.      4.OA.4 | 14.      4.MD.6 <br> W, S, A | 15.      4.G.1 |

# Lesson #53

1.   The coffee shop served 4 times as many hot coffees as iced coffees.  They served 7 iced coffees.  How many hot coffees did they serve?

2.   Janet and Sadie have 40 minutes for lunch.  When they went out to lunch, it took an hour and 2 minutes.  How many minutes late were Janet and Sadie getting back from lunch?

3.   Find the measure of $\angle NOP$.

4.   $360 \div 9 = ?$

5.   Round 4,331 to the nearest thousand.

6.   **One liter (l) is 1,000 milliliters (mL).**  Write 1 liter $= 1,000$ mL in the box.

7.   If $\angle T$ is a right angle, what is the measure of $d$?

8.   $55 \times 14 = ?$  Complete the matrix model to find the product.

9.   The perimeter of this rectangle is 36 m.  The length is given. Find the width.   Remember to label your answer.

$l = 11\,m$

$perimeter = 36\,m$

10.   $2,682 \bigcirc 2,826$

11.   Choose the sign that makes this sentence true.  Think about this: $\dfrac{40}{100} = \dfrac{4}{10} = \dfrac{2}{5}$
Which has more fifths, $\dfrac{2}{5}$ or $\dfrac{3}{5}$?

12.   Describe the pattern.   5, 13, 21, 29, 37

13.   $5,377 + 4,264 = ?$

14.   $10,566 - 6,497 = ?$

15.   Myles was at soccer practice for 3 hours this week. Rafiq was at practice 4 times as long.  How long was Rafiq at practice?   Complete the number sentence.

| 1.          4.OA.1 | 2.          4.MD.2 | 3.          4.MD.6 |
|---|---|---|

| 4.          4.NBT.6 | 5.          4.NBT.3 | 6.          4.MD.1 |
|---|---|---|

| 7.          4.MD.7 | 8.          4.NBT.5 | 9.          4.MD.3 |
|---|---|---|

| 10.          4.NBT.2 | 11.          4.NF.2 | 12.          4.OA.5 |
|---|---|---|

**11.**

$$\frac{40}{100} \bigcirc \frac{3}{5}$$

| 13.          4.NBT.4 | 14.          4.NBT.4 | 15.          4.OA.2 |
|---|---|---|

**15.**

| Rafiq | ? | | | |
|---|---|---|---|---|
| Miles | 3 | 3 | 3 | 3 |

_____ × _____ = _____

# Lesson #54

1. Marco is riding his bicycle from Columbus, OH, to Chicago, IL. The entire trip is 357 miles. He makes it there in 6 days. He traveled 60 miles on day one, 60 on day two, 65 on day three, 55 on day four, and 60 on day five. Write an equation that would show how to find his mileage on day six.

2. $3,568 + 9,862 = ?$

3. If $\angle PWL$ is a straight angle, what is the measure of $a$?

4. Write another equivalent fraction for $\frac{1}{5}$.

5. The wall near the school office is 3 meters wide. Mr. Kent separated the wall into 4 equal sections. How many centimeters wide is each section?

6. Which lines are parallel?    A)    B)    C) 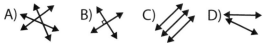   D)

7. $62 \times 51 =$ \_\_\_\_\_ Complete the matrix model to find the product.

8. Write 2,485 in expanded form.

9. $2,000 =$ \_\_\_\_\_ $\times 10$

10. Is the measure of $\angle BIT$ most likely to be 20°, 90°, or 130°?

11. $9,423 - 5,279 = ?$

12. One liter (l) equals \_\_\_\_\_ milliliters (mL).

13. The perimeter of this rectangle is 22 cm. The length is given. Find the width. Remember to label your answer.

    $l = 9\,cm$

    perimeter = 22 cm

14. Round 32,367 to the nearest ten thousand.

15. An angle that turns through $\frac{1}{360}$ of a circle is called a "one-degree angle" and can be used to measure angles. What type of angle turns through $\frac{1}{360}$ of a circle?

| 1. 4.OA.3 | 2. 4.NBT.4 | 3. 4.MD.7 |
|---|---|---|
| | | 129° $a°$ <br> P    W    L |
| **4. 4.NF.1** <br><br> $\dfrac{1}{5} = \dfrac{2}{10} = \dfrac{\square}{\square}$ | **5. 4.MD.2** | **6. 4.G.1** |
| **7. 4.NBT.5** <br><br> ___ + ___ <br> ___ + ___ | **8. 4.NBT.2** | **9. 4.NBT.1** |
| **10. 4.MD.6** <br><br> T <br> B    I | **11. 4.NBT.4** | **12. 4.MD.1** |
| **13. 4.MD.3** | **14. 4.NBT.3** | **15. 4.MD.5** |

# Lesson #55

1.  The perimeter of this rectangle is 20mm. The width is given. Find the length. Remember to label your answer.

*perimeter = 20 mm*     $w = 3$ mm

2.  Use the distributive property to multiply $5,745 \times 4$. Find the product.

3.  If 1,000 mL = 1 liter, then 2,000 mL = _____ liters.

4.  $560 \div 7 = ?$

5.  $52 \times 35 = ?$ Complete the matrix model to find the product.

6.  $4,900 - 2,713 = ?$

7.  Round 33,414 to the nearest thousand.

8.  Find all the factor pairs for 49.

9.  Find the measure of $\angle OPQ$.

10. Lloyd caught 15 fish at the river today. That is 13 more than his son, Jim, caught. How many fish did Jim catch? Choose the correct equation and solve it.

11. $6,451 + 8,367 = ?$

12. Draw an obtuse angle. Label it $\angle DEF$.

line of symmetry

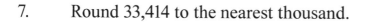

13. Draw a circle. Show at least four different lines of symmetry.

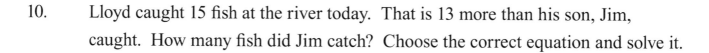

14. Fill in the denominator to show an equivalent fraction.

15. Write 2,412 using words.

| 1.     4.MD.3 | 2.     4.NBT.5 | 3.     4.MD.1 |
|---|---|---|
| 4.     4.NBT.6 | 5.     4.NBT.5 | 6.     4.NBT.4 |
| 7.     4.NBT.3 | 8.     4.OA.4 | 9.     4.MD.6 |
| 10.     4.OA.2 <br><br> A) $13 + 15 = f$ <br><br> B) $13 + f = 15$ | 11.     4.NBT.4 | 12.     4.G.1 |
| 13.     4.G.3 | 14.     4.NF.2 <br><br> $$\frac{2}{6} = \frac{4}{\Box}$$ | 15.     4.NBT.2 |

# Lesson #56

1. $49 \times 18 = ?$ Complete the matrix model to find the product.

2. If $\angle TLO$ is a right angle, what is the measure of $e$?

3. $4,456 \div 5 = ?$ See *Help Pages* for place value model.

4. Fill in the numerator to show an equivalent fraction.

5. $12,866 \bigcirc 12,668$

6. Is 35 prime or composite? Explain.

7. Carrie filled the tub with 10 liters of water to bathe her dog. How many milliliters of water did Carrie use?

8. Two lines are perpendicular if they intersect and form a right angle (90°). Which pair of lines is perpendicular?

9. $10 \times 98 = 980$ because the 9 in 980 represents 9 hundreds, which is _____ times as much as 9 tens, and the 8 in 980 represents 8 tens, which is _____ times as much as 8 ones.

10. $24,685 + 16,988 = ?$

11. Is $\angle PTO$ acute, right, or obtuse?

12. Write the base-ten number for $8,000 + 500 + 60 + 1$.

13. Some numbers add up to 400, but one of the numbers is missing. Which equation shows how to find the missing number?

14. Describe the pattern. 4, 8, 12, 16, 20

15. Sheryl put 112 liters of water in the bathtub to give her little sister a bath. Her sister splashed so much that there were only $110\frac{1}{2}$ liters left in the tub after the bath. How many milliliters of water were splashed out of the tub?

**1.**   4.NBT.5

$$\_\_\_ + \_\_\_$$
$$\_\_\_ + \_\_\_$$

**2.**   4.MD.7

$e°$   $52°$
T, L, O

**3.**   4.NBT.6

**4.**   4.NF.1

$$\frac{6}{8} = \frac{\square}{4}$$

**5.**   4.NBT.2

**6.**   4.OA.4

**7.**   4.MD.1

**8.**   4.G.1

A)   B)   C)   D)

**9.**   4.NBT.1

**10.**   4.NBT.4

**11.**   4.G.1

T, O, P

**12.**   4.NBT.2

**13.**   4.OA.3

A) $89 + 17 + 120 + 167 + 400 = x$

B) $x = 400 - 89 - 17 - 120 - 167$

**14.**   4.OA.5

**15.**   4.MD.2

# Lesson #57

1.    5,243 ◯ 5,432

2.    Which shows the use of the distributive property for 4,395 × 5?

3.    The perimeter of this rectangle is 26 cm.
      The width is given.  Find the length.
      Remember to label your answer.

      | perimeter = 26 cm | 3 cm |

4.    Fill in the sign that makes this sentence true.

5.    4,862 ÷ 2 = ?

6.    Is the measure of $\angle PIG$ most likely to be 15°, 45°, or 75°?

7.    57 × 48 = ?  Complete the matrix model to find the product.

8.    Mrs. Yu brought a 4-liter jug of water for the soccer team.  The first player
      drank 500 milliliters.  How many milliliters were left in the jug that Mrs. Yu
      brought?

9.    If $\angle RDB$ is a straight angle, what is the measure of $x$?

10.   Round 42,802 to the nearest ten thousand.

11.   In Cleveland, Ohio, the average amount of rain in February is
      about 2 inches.  In September, it is 2 times that amount.
      On average, how many inches of rain does Cleveland
      get in September?  Complete the number sentence.

12.   6,000 − 2,335 = ?

13.   23,465 + 19,788 = ?

14.   List the first 10 multiples of 8.

15.   Tom's dart hit the target's red bullseye from 3.5 meters
      away.  How many centimeters away was Tom?

| | | |
|---|---|---|
| **1.**　4.NBT.2 | **2.**　4.NBT.5<br><br>A) $(4{,}000 \times 5) + (300 \times 5) + (900 \times 5) + (5 \times 5)$<br><br>B) $(4{,}000 \times 5) + (300 \times 5) + (90 \times 5) + (5 \times 5)$ | **3.**　4.MD.3 |
| **4.**　4.NF.2<br><br>$\dfrac{7}{8} \bigcirc \dfrac{6}{8}$ | **5.**　4.NBT.6 | **6.**　4.MD.6 |
| **7.**　4.NBT.5 | **8.**　4.MD.2 | **9.**　4.MD.7 |
| **10.**　4.NBT.3 | **11.**　4.OA.2<br><br>_____ × _____ = _____ | **12.**　4.NBT.4 |
| **13.**　4.NBT.4 | **14.**　4.OA.4 | **15.**　4.MD.1 |

# Lesson #58

1.   Round 14,325 to the nearest hundred.

2.   If $\angle K$ is a right angle, what is the measure of $u$?

3.   Henry's book bag weighed 7 kilograms.  How many grams did it weigh?

4.   Draw $\overline{ST}$ in the box.

5.   $61 \times 36 = ?$  Complete the matrix model to find the product.

6.   The perimeter of this rectangle is 18 in.  The length is 5 in.  Find the width.
     Remember to label your answer.

7.   18 is a multiple of 1, 2, 3, _____, _____, and _____.

8.   Write another equivalent fraction for $\frac{2}{4}$.

9.   Juanita is collecting money for the local community center.  Her goal for the
     week is $600.  Her counts for Monday–Saturday are $65, $115, $98, $47, $66,
     and $99.  Which equation shows how to find the amount she must make on
     Sunday to reach her goal?

10.  If a waiter has a 2-liter pitcher of water and fills each glass with 250 milliliters
     of water, how many glasses will he be able to fill before the pitcher is empty?

11.  $3,443 + 6,588 = ?$

12.  Describe the pattern.     5, 11, 17, 23, 29

13.  $8,652 - 1,593 = ?$

14.  Find the measure of $\angle OPQ$.

15.  Floyd found 63 shells at the beach on Thursday.  That is 7 times more than he
     found on Tuesday.  Choose the best equation and use it to find out how many
     shells Floyd found on Tuesday.

| | | |
|---|---|---|
| **1.** 4.NBT.3 | **2.** 4.MD.7 | **3.** 4.MD.1 |
| **4.** 4.G.1 | **5.** 4.NBT.5 | **6.** 4.MD.3 5 in. perimeter = 18 in. |
| **7.** 4.OA.4 | **8.** 4.NF.1 $$\frac{2}{4} = \frac{4}{8} = \frac{\square}{\square}$$ | **9.** 4.OA.3 A) $65 + 115 + 98 + 47 + 66 + 99 - y = 600$ B) $600 - 65 - 115 - 98 - 47 - 66 - 99 = x$ |
| **10.** 4.MD.2 | **11.** 4.NBT.4 | **12.** 4.OA.5 |
| **13.** 4.NBT.4 | **14.** 4.MD.6 | **15.** 4.OA.2 A) $7 \times s = 63$ B) $7 \times 63 = s$ |

# Lesson #59

1.   $3,921 + 9,822 = ?$

2.   If $\angle TXV$ is a straight angle, what is the measure of $g$?

3.   $8,424 \div 4 = ?$

4.   Jerry needs to make several hundred hot dogs for a party. He asks his neighbors to help him. Rhonda makes 127, Louis makes 183, Consuela makes 217, and Michel makes 93. Jerry himself makes 300. How many hot dogs were made altogether?

5.   Find all the factor pairs for 24.

6.   $3,789 \bigcirc 3,798$

7.   $3,814 - 1,897 = ?$

8.   The boys were filling a pool for the puppy to play in. Sam poured $2\frac{1}{2}$ liters of water into the pool. Jeff added 3 liters, and Will poured in 850 milliliters of water. Altogether, how many milliliters of water was put into the pool?

9.   Choose the sign that makes this sentence true. Think about this: $\frac{60}{100} = \frac{6}{10} = \frac{3}{5}$. Which has more fifths, $\frac{3}{5}$ or $\frac{4}{5}$?

10.  $61 \times 34 = ?$   Complete the matrix model to find the product.

11.  Round 5,062 to the nearest hundred.

12.  There were 6 times as many catfish in the lake as trout. There were 5 trout in the lake. How many catfish were in the lake?

13.  Bobbi drank 1 liter of iced tea. How many milliliters of tea did Bobbi drink?

14.  Which shows the use of the distributive property for $6,216 \times 7$?

15.  An angle that turns through 80 one-degree angles has a measure of 80°. An angle that turns through 42 one-degree angles has a measure of _____.

| | | |
|---|---|---|
| **1.**   4.NBT.4 | **2.**   4.MD.7 | **3.**   4.NBT.6 |
| **4.**   4.OA.3 Make it easier by using compatible numbers! | **5.**   4.OA.4 | **6.**   4.NBT.2 |
| **7.**   4.NBT.4 | **8.**   4.MD.2 | **9.**   4.NF.2 $$\frac{60}{100} \bigcirc \frac{4}{5}$$ |
| **10.**   4.NBT.5 | **11.**   4.NBT.3 | **12.**   4.OA.1 |
| **13.**   4.MD.1 | **14.**   4.NBT.5 <br><br> A) $(6{,}000 \times 7) + (2{,}000 \times 7) + (10 \times 7) + (6 \times 7)$ <br><br> B) $(6{,}000 \times 7) + (200 \times 7) + (10 \times 7) + (6 \times 7)$ | **15.**   4.MD.5 |

# Lesson #60

1.    Draw ray *AD*.

2.    $6{,}000 - 4{,}213 = ?$

3.    **One pound (lb) is 16 ounces (oz).**  Write 1 lb = 16 oz in the box.

4.    $720 \div 8 = ?$

5.    Micah spotted 3 times as many birds
      today than he spotted yesterday.
      Yesterday he spotted 9 birds.
      How many birds did Micah spot today?

6.    Write 25,314 in expanded form.

7.    Write another equivalent fraction for $\frac{1}{3}$.

8.    Is 64 prime or composite?  Explain.

9.    The perimeter of this rectangle is 28 in.  The length is
      given.  Find the width.  Remember to label your answer.

      9 in.

      perimeter = 28 in.

10.   $42{,}413 + 36{,}586 = ?$

11.   Draw a hexagon.  Show at least four different lines of symmetry.

12.   $45 \times 15 = ?$  Complete the matrix model to find the product.

13.   Melissa talked on the phone for 6 hours this month.  Her big sister, Erin, talked
      3 times as many hours as Melissa did.  How many hours did Erin spend on the
      phone? Complete the number sentence.

14.   Harry wants to drive from Chicago to New York City in 4 days.  It will take him
      about 12 hours and 24 minutes to do this.   How many minutes each day will he
      spend driving?

15.   If $\angle FGH$ is a right angle, what is the measure of *t*?

| | | |
|---|---|---|
| **1.**   4.G.1 | **2.**   4.NBT.4 | **3.**   4.MD.1 |
| **4.**   4.NBT.6 | **5.**   4.OA.1 | **6.**   4.NBT.2 |
| **7.**   4.NF.1 $$\frac{1}{3} = \frac{2}{6} = \frac{\square}{\square}$$ | **8.**   4.OA.4 | **9.**   4.MD.3 |
| **10.**   4.NBT.4 | **11.**   4.G.3 | **12.**   4.NBT.5 |
| **13.**   4.OA.2 | **14.**   4.MD.2 | **15.**   4.MD.7 |

**13.**

| Erin | ? | | |
|---|---|---|---|
| Melissa | 6 | 6 | 6 |

_____ × _____ = _____

**15.** 

F, 49°, $t°$, G, H

# Lesson #61

1.    Write 300,000 + 60,000 + 7,000 + 400 + 6 as a base-ten number.

2.    Which shows the use of the distributive property for 2,674 × 9?

3.    Which lines are parallel?

4.    One pound (lb) equals _____ ounces.

5.    Fill in the sign that makes this sentence true.  Think about this: $\frac{9}{12} = \frac{3}{4}$.

6.    If ∠XOP is a straight angle, what is the measure of k?

7.    Dolly the dolphin can jump 11 feet high.  Her trainer wants her to jump $13\frac{1}{2}$ feet high.  How many more inches does Dolly need to jump to reach the goal?

8.    Is 59 prime or composite?  Explain.

9.    28 × 28 = ?  Complete the matrix model to find the product.

10.   Describe the pattern.  2, 5, 8, 11, 14
      Are the numbers always even, always odd, or do they alternate?

11.   3,906 ÷ 3 = ?

12.   Circle the triangle that has a right angle.

13.   743 − 259 = ?

14.   Sanjay has decided to put $175 a week from his paycheck into a savings account.  For every $175 Sanjay puts away, his company adds $25.  After 20 weeks of saving, Sanjay must take $240 out of savings for a car repair.  How much is left in his savings account after the repair?

15.   Is the measure of ∠PUT most likely to be 70°, 90°, or 110°?

| | | |
|---|---|---|
| **1.**      4.NBT.2 | **2.**      4.NBT.5 <br><br> A) $(2{,}000 \times 9) + (60 \times 9) + (70 \times 9) + (4 \times 9)$ <br><br> B) $(2{,}000 \times 9) + (600 \times 9) + (70 \times 9) + (4 \times 9)$ | **3.**      4.G.1 |
| **4.**      4.MD.1 | **5.**      4.NF.2 <br><br> $$\frac{9}{12} \bigcirc \frac{2}{4}$$ | **6.**      4.MD.7 <br> |
| **7.**      4.MD.2 | **8.**      4.OA.4 | **9.**      4.NBT.5 <br> |
| **10.**      4.OA.5 | **11.**      4.NBT.6 | **12.**      4.G.2 <br> |
| **13.**      4.NBT.4 | **14.**      4.OA.3 | **15.**      4.MD.6 <br> |

# Lesson #62

1.  **Area is the size of a surface.  Area is always expressed in square units (Example: square meters or m².).  Multiply the length by the width to find the area of a rectangle ($l \times w$).**  What is the area of this rectangle? Label your answer.

2.  The Traverse family is taking a 900-mile trip.  The parents drive in shifts. Tammi drives 2 shifts; one is 198 miles and the other is 189 miles.  Ted's shifts are 105 miles and 202 miles.  If there are about 200 miles left to go, Tammi will drive.  If about 100, Ted will drive.  Write an equation to represent the problem using the letter $x$ for the unknown number.  Who will be driving?

3.  $60,000 - 24,566 = ?$

4.  Two lines are perpendicular if they intersect and form a right angle (90°). Which lines are perpendicular?

    A) B) C) D)

5.  If 1 lb = 16 oz, then 2 lb = _____ oz.

6.  Write another equivalent fraction for $\frac{1}{2}$.

7.  If $\angle Z$ is a right angle, what is the measure of $a$?

8.  $3,632 \div 4 = ?$

9.  Corey traded twice as many baseball cards today as he traded yesterday. Yesterday he traded 5 cards.  How many cards did Corey trade today?

10.  Is the measure of $\angle TOE$ most likely to be 10°, 35°, or 65°?

11.  $52 \times 43 = ?$   Complete the matrix model to find the product.

12.  Write the number 3,077 using words.

13.  List the first 10 multiples of 7.

14.  Describe the pattern.  3, 7, 11, 15, 19
     Are the numbers always even, always odd, or do they alternate?

15.  Claire put 15 fireflies in a jar.  That is 6 more than her sister, Emma, put in her jar.  How many fireflies does Emma have in her jar?  Choose the correct equation and solve it.

**1.**      4.MD.3

10 mm

8 mm

**2.**      4.OA.3

**3.**      4.NBT.4

**4.**      4.G.1

**5.**      4.MD.1

**6.**      4.NF.1

$$\frac{1}{2} = \frac{3}{6} = \frac{\square}{\square}$$

**7.**      4.MD.7

$a°$

$55°$

Z

**8.**      4.NBT.6

**9.**      4.OA.1

**10.**      4.MD.6

T

O     E

**11.**      4.NBT.5

+

____ + ____

**12.**      4.NBT.2

**13.**      4.OA.4

**14.**      4.OA.5

**15.**      4.OA.2

A)   $15 + 6 = f$

B)   $6 + f = 15$

# Lesson #63

1. Beckett's class raised $30 for the city food bank. Reagan's class raised 5 times that amount. How much money did Reagan's class raise for the city food bank? Write a number sentence and solve it.

2. Write 32,412 in expanded form.

3. $5,000 - 1,997 = ?$

4. Round 1,652 to the nearest hundred.

5. $10 \times 67 = 670$ because the 6 in 670 represents 6 hundreds, which is _____ times as much as 6 tens, and the 7 in 670 represents 7 tens, which is _____ times as much as 7 ones.

6. $16,342 + 8,465 = ?$

7. What is the area of this rectangle? Label the answer.

8. Althea is making sugar cookies for her class. Her recipe calls for 900 grams of sugar, $1\frac{1}{2}$ kilograms of flour, 22 grams of baking powder, and 9 grams of salt. How many grams of these ingredients are used?

9. Describe the pattern. 2, 12, 22, 32, 42

10. 15 is a multiple of 1, _____, _____, and 15.

11. A package of printer paper weighs 5 pounds. How many ounces does it weigh?

12. The video rental kiosk rented out 125 videos on Monday, 134 on Tuesday, 75 on Wednesday, and 76 on Thursday. If the kiosk has the same number of rentals over the next four days, how many total videos will have been rented?

13. $59 \times 32 = ?$ Complete the matrix model to find the product.

14. $2,505 \div 5 = ?$

15. When comparing fractions with like denominators, simply compare the numerators. Fill in the sign that makes this sentence true.

**1.**      4.OA.2

| Reagan's class | ? | | | | |
|---|---|---|---|---|---|
| Beckett's class | 30 | 30 | 30 | 30 | 30 |

**2.**      4.NBT.2

**3.**      4.NBT.4

**4.**      4.NBT.3

**5.**      4.NBT.1

**6.**      4.NBT.4

**7.**      4.MD.3

7 in.

3 in.

**8.**      4.MD.2

**9.**      4.OA.5

**10.**      4.OA.4

**11.**      4.MD.1

**12.**      4.OA.3

**13.**      4.NBT.5

_____
_____ +
_____ + _____

**14.**      4.NBT.6

**15.**      4.NF.2

$$\frac{6}{8} \bigcirc \frac{7}{8}$$

# Lesson #64

1. $13{,}246 + 14{,}589 = ?$

2. An angle that turns through 67 one-degree angles has a measure of _____.

3. $35 \times 22 = ?$ Complete the matrix model to find the product.

4. Martine travels to several daycare centers to teach art every week. She sees 200 students in all. On Monday, she sees 67 students, on Tuesday, she sees 44, on Wednesday, she sees 33. Martine does not work on Friday, so how many students must she see Thursday? Write an equation and solve it.

5. Fill in the numerator to show an equivalent fraction.

6. What is the area of this rectangle? Label the answer.

7. $1{,}000 - 855 = ?$

8. Two lines are parallel if they never intersect and are always the same distance apart. A) B) C) D) Which lines are parallel?

9. Jazzy rode her bike 16 miles this week. That is 8 times as many miles as she rode last week. Choose the best equation and use it to find out how far she rode last week.

10. If $\angle DSB$ is a straight angle, what is the measure of $y$?

11. Sam made 3 times as many baskets in today's game than last week's. Last week he made 9 baskets. How many baskets did he make this week?

12. $6{,}824 \div 4 = ?$

13. Marcia divided the peanut butter fudge into sections of 1.5 kg each. How many grams did each section of fudge weigh?

14. Find the measure of $\angle DEF$.

15. Round 55,006 to the nearest thousand.

| 1.      4.NBT.4 | 2.      4.MD.5 | 3.      4.NBT.5 |
|---|---|---|
|  |  | |
| 4.      4.OA.3 | 5.      4.NF.1 | 6.      4.MD.3 |
|  | $$\frac{2}{12} = \frac{\square}{6}$$ | 9 m, 4 m |
| 7.      4.NBT.4 | 8.      4.G.1 | 9.      4.OA.2 <br> A) $8 \times 16 = m$ <br> B) $8 \times m = 16$ |
| 10.      4.MD.7 <br> | 11.      4.OA.1 | 12.      4.NBT.6 |
| 13.      4.MD.1 | 14.      4.MD.6 <br> | 15.      4.NBT.3 |

# Lesson #65

1.    $4,000 - 2,475 = ?$

2.    If the two rays form a right angle, what is the value of $a$?

3.    Is 24 prime or composite? Explain.

4.    Round 42,316 to the nearest ten thousand.

5.    What is the area of a rectangle with a length of 7 cm
      and a width of 3 cm? Label the answer.

6.    $32,488 + 19,596 = ?$

7.    Jamie rode the roller coaster 15 times this year. That is 3 times as often as
      his sister, Taylor, rode it. How many times did Taylor ride the roller coaster?
      Choose the correct equation and solve it.

8.    Two lines are perpendicular if they intersect
      and form a right angle (90°). Which lines are
      perpendicular?

9.    Which shows the use of the distributive property for $6,573 \times 5$?

10.   The larger the denominator, the smaller the unit is. Fill in the sign that makes
      this sentence true.

11.   Nina baked cookies for the party. The recipe called for 1 kilogram of flour, 195
      grams of brown sugar, 450 grams of chopped nuts, and 670 grams of chocolate
      chips. How many grams of ingredients were used?

12.   $2,525 \div 5 = ?$

13.   Is $\angle SRL$ acute, right, or obtuse?

14.   $72 \times 13 = ?$ Complete the matrix model to find the product.

15.   The steak weighed 12 ounces. Did the steak weigh more or less than a pound?

| | | |
|---|---|---|
| **1.** 4.NBT.4 | **2.** 4.MD.7 | **3.** 4.OA.4 |
| **4.** 4.NBT.3 | **5.** 4.MD.3 | **6.** 4.NBT.4 |
| **7.** 4.OA.2 <br><br> A) $3 + r = 15$ <br><br> B) $3 \times r = 15$ | **8.** 4.G.1 | **9.** 4.NBT.5 <br><br> A) $(6{,}000 \times 5) + (500 \times 5) + (70 \times 5) + (3 \times 5)$ <br><br> B) $(6{,}000 \times 50) + (500 \times 5) + (70 \times 5) + (3 \times 5)$ |
| **10.** 4.NF.2 <br><br> $\dfrac{7}{8} \bigcirc \dfrac{7}{12}$ | **11.** 4.MD.2 | **12.** 4.NBT.6 |
| **13.** 4.G.1 | **14.** 4.NBT.5 | **15.** 4.MD.1 |

# Lesson #66

1.  Judy wrote in her journal for a half hour on Monday, Tuesday, Wednesday, and Thursday. How many minutes did Judy spend writing?

2.  Round 476 to the nearest ten.

3.  For this equation, which of the following is the best estimate for $x$: 300, 400, or 500?

4.  $\overrightarrow{BA}$ and $\overrightarrow{BC}$ are perpendicular. What is the value of $g$?

5.  $5,376 \div 4 = ?$

6.  Which shows a line of symmetry?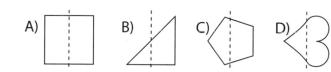

7.  $62,345 + 36,274 = ?$

8.  Which lines are parallel?

9.  $61 \times 31 = ?$ Complete the matrix model to find the product.

10. What is the area of this rectangle? Label the answer.

11. List the first 10 multiples of 10.

12. Describe the pattern. 7, 10, 13, 16, 19
    Are the numbers always even, always odd, or do they alternate?

13. The television remote control works up to 6 feet away from the TV. Billy is sitting in the kitchen and is $7\frac{1}{2}$ feet away from the TV. How many inches closer to the TV must Billy get for the remote control to work?

14. Write $60,000 + 7,000 + 400 + 80 + 2$ as a base-ten number.

15. Is the measure of $\angle WIT$ most likely to be 25°, 50°, or 75°?

| 1. 4.MD.1 | 2. 4.NBT.3 | 3. 4.OA.3 |
|---|---|---|
| | | $$105 + 89 + 115 + 85 = x$$ |

| 4. 4.MD.7 | 5. 4.NBT.6 | 6. 4.G.3 |
|---|---|---|
| | | |

| 7. 4.NBT.4 | 8. 4.G.1 | 9. 4.NBT.5 |
|---|---|---|
| | | |

| 10. 4.MD.3 | 11. 4.OA.4 | 12. 4.OA.5 |
|---|---|---|
| | | |

| 13. 4.MD.2 | 14. 4.NBT.2 | 15. 4.MD.6 |
|---|---|---|
| | | |

# Lesson #67

1.      $37 \times 51 = ?$  Use a matrix model to find the product.

2.      $6,000 - 3,444 = ?$

3.      Round 86,413 to the nearest thousand.

4.      If $\angle ABC$ and $\angle CBD$ are right angles, what is the value of $n$?

5.      Which shows the use of the distributive property for $8,943 \times 7$?

6.      Nia practiced the piano for 30 hours in January.  That is 5 times as many hours as she practiced in December.  Choose the best equation and use it to find out how many hours she practiced in December.

7.      $4,842 \div 2 = ?$

8.      Draw an obtuse angle.

9.      Ruthie has four banks full of quarters.  She empties each out onto the floor and counts them.  Bank One has 98 quarters, Bank Two has 77, Bank Three has 21, and Bank Four has 10.  Ruthie wants to save 250 quarters in all.  How many quarters does she still need to save?

10.     Mr. Hiller bought 2,000 grams of coffee.  How many kilograms of coffee did he buy?

11.     $5,218 + 6,970 = ?$

12.     9 is a multiple of 1, _____, and _____.

13.     Find the measure of $\angle KLM$.

14.     Describe the pattern.  4, 8, 12, 16, 20

        Are the numbers always even, always odd, or do they alternate?

15.     When comparing fractions with like denominators, simply compare the numerators.  Fill in the sign that makes this sentence true.

| | | |
|---|---|---|
| **1.** 4.NBT.5 | **2.** 4.NBT.4 | **3.** 4.NBT.3 |
| **4.** 4.MD.7 | **5.** 4.NBT.5<br><br>A) $(8{,}000 \times 7) + (900 \times 7) + (40 \times 7) + (3 \times 7)$<br><br>B) $(800 \times 7) + (900 \times 7) + (40 \times 7) + (3 \times 7)$ | **6.** 4.OA.2<br><br>A) $5 \times h = 30$<br><br>B) $5 \times 30 = h$ |
| **7.** 4.NBT.6 | **8.** 4.G.1 | **9.** 4.OA.3 |
| **10.** 4.MD.1 | **11.** 4.NBT.4 | **12.** 4.OA.4 |
| **13.** 4.MD.6 | **14.** 4.OA.5 | **15.** 4.NF.2<br><br>$\dfrac{5}{8} \bigcirc \dfrac{5}{8}$ |

# Lesson #68

1.      $18,605 - 3,278 = ?$

2.      Jillian drank a 2-liter bottle of fruit punch and a 355-milliliter can of fruit punch
        in one day.  In milliliters, how much fruit punch did Jillian drink?

3.      Junebug is making a cube out of large marshmallows.  She wants an
        $8 \times 8 \times 8$ marshmallow cube, which means she needs 512 marshmallows.  She
        already has 320 marshmallows.  Choose the equation that will tell her how many
        more marshmallows she needs.

4.      Round 156,213 to the nearest ten thousand.

5.      $50 \div 8 = ?$

6.      $42 \times 53 = ?$  Use a matrix model to find the product.

7.      Find all the factor pairs for 30.

8.      Is $\angle ZWM$ acute, right, or obtuse?

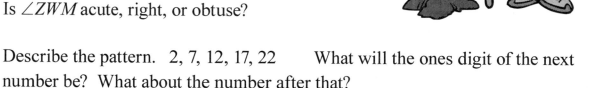

9.      Describe the pattern.  2, 7, 12, 17, 22        What will the ones digit of the next
        number be?  What about the number after that?

10.     Jamie bought 1 pound of salt for his mother.  How many ounces did the salt
        weigh?

11.     $500 = \_\_\_\_\_$ tens

12.     $26,337 + 49,412 = ?$

13.     Draw perpendicular lines.

14.     Fill in the denominator to show an equivalent fraction.

15.     Milan was working on her Science Fair project.  Her plant was 53 cm tall today.
        That was 12 cm taller than it was last week.  How tall was Milan's plant last
        week?  Choose the correct equation and solve it.

| 1.    4.NBT.4 | 2.    4.MD.2 | 3.    4.OA.3 |
|---|---|---|
| | | A) $512 - 320 = y$ <br><br> B) $320 \times 8 - 512 = y$ |
| 4.    4.NBT.3 | 5.    3.OA.7 | 6.    4.NBT.5 <br><br> |
| 7.    4.OA.4 | 8.    4.G.1 <br><br> | 9.    4.OA.5 |
| 10.    4.MD.1 | 11.    4.NBT.1 | 12.    4.NBT.4 |
| 13.    4.G.1 | 14.    4.NF.1 <br><br> $$\frac{2}{12} = \frac{1}{\square}$$ | 15.    4.OA.2 <br><br> A) $12 + p = 53$ <br><br> B) $12 + 53 = p$ |

# Lesson #69

1. $3,865 + 4,919 = ?$

2. If the two rays form a right angle, what is the value of $p$?

3. $4,000 - 1,650 = ?$

4. Compare the unit fractions to the right. The larger the denominator, the smaller the unit is. Fill in the sign that makes this sentence true.

   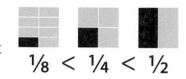

   $\frac{1}{8} < \frac{1}{4} < \frac{1}{2}$

5. Which shows the use of the distributive property for $1,547 \times 9$?

6. Round 14,236 to the nearest hundred.

7. Describe the pattern.

8. Is the measure of $\angle PAW$ most likely to be 30°, 60°, or 90°?

9. Stacey jumped off the diving board that was 60 inches high. How many feet high was the diving board?

10. Each morning, the science club sold orange juice to raise money for lab supplies. On Friday, the club began with $4\frac{1}{2}$ liters of juice. The members sold 3,503 milliliters. How many milliliters of juice were left over?

11. $180 \div 3 = ?$

12. Is 32 prime or composite? Explain.

13. $23 \times 46 = ?$ Use a matrix model to find the product.

14. $5,000 = \underline{\hspace{1cm}}$ hundreds

15. Jason sold 12 candy bars for his band field trip. Debi sold 3 times that amount. How many candy bars did Debi sell? Write a number sentence and solve it.

| | | |
|---|---|---|
| **1.**    4.NBT.4 | **2.**    4.MD.7 | **3.**    4.NBT.4 |
| **4.**    4.NF.2 $$\frac{4}{5} \bigcirc \frac{4}{10}$$ | **5.**    4.NBT.5 <br><br> A) $(1 \times 900) + (500 \times 9) + (40 \times 9) + (7 \times 9)$ <br><br> B) $(1{,}000 \times 9) + (500 \times 9) + (40 \times 9) + (7 \times 9)$ | **6.**    4.NBT.3 |
| **7.**    4.OA.5 | **8.**    4.MD.6 | **9.**    4.MD.1 |
| **10.**    4.MD.2 | **11.**    4.NBT.6 | **12.**    4.OA.4 |
| **13.**    4.NBT.5 | **14.**    4.NBT.1 | **15.**    4.OA.2 |

# Lesson #70

1.      $3,458 + 8,765 = ?$

2.      Draw a line of symmetry for each shape.  Cross out the shape that has no line of symmetry.

3.      Write two equivalent fractions for $\frac{1}{8}$.

4.      Describe the pattern.

5.      $1,824 \div 3 = ?$

6.      List the first 10 multiples of 4.

7.      $\overrightarrow{ZX}$ and $\overrightarrow{ZY}$ are perpendicular.  What is the value of $r$?

8.      Paula needs 550 acrylic press-on nails.  She goes to four local stores.  She got 55 from store one, 95 from store two, and 135 from store three.  Before she gets to store four, she finds a box of 100 in her trunk.  How many nails must she get from store four to reach 550 nails?

9.      $36,205 - 18,658 = ?$

10.     Which shape has parallel sides?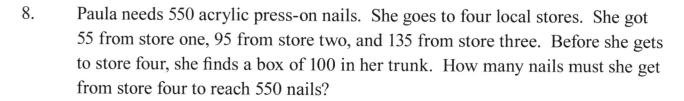

11.     $81 \times 14 = ?$  Use a matrix model to find the product.

12.     Round 76 to the nearest ten.

13.     Rena made 72 favors for her sister's wedding.  That is 9 times as many as she made yesterday.  Choose the best equation and use it to find out how many favors she put together yesterday.

14.     A row of tulips is 4.5 meters long.  How many centimeters long is the row of tulips?

15.     Is $\angle FLC$ acute, right, or obtuse?

| | | |
|---|---|---|
| **1.**     4.NBT.4 | **2.**     4.G.3 | **3.**     4.NF.1 $$\frac{1}{8} = \frac{\square}{\square} = \frac{\square}{\square}$$ |
| **4.**     4.OA.5 | **5.**     4.NBT.6 | **6.**     4.OA.4 |
| **7.**     4.MD.7 | **8.**     4.OA.3 | **9.**     4.NBT.4 |
| **10.**     4.G.2 | **11.**     4.NBT.5 | **12.**     4.NBT.3 |
| **13.**     4.OA.2 <br><br> A) $9 \times f = 72$ <br><br> B) $72 \times 9 = f$ | **14.**     4.MD.1 | **15.**     4.G.1 |

# Lesson #71

1. Aaron was building with his building blocks. He built a tower that was 73 blocks high. That was 14 blocks taller than his tower was yesterday. How tall was his building yesterday? Choose the correct equation and solve it.

2. Two lines are parallel if they never intersect and are always the same distance apart. Draw $\overleftrightarrow{QR}$ parallel to $\overleftrightarrow{ST}$ in the box.

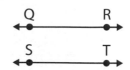

3. Round 54,210 to the nearest thousand.

4. $15,264 + 8,366 = ?$

5. $60,000 = $ _____ thousands

6. Use a matrix model to find the product: $72 \times 25 = ?$

7. The Burger Barn sells 120 burgers a day on weekdays and 180 a day on weekends. Which of the following is the best estimate for how many burgers they sell in a week: 600, 800, or 1,000?

8. Fill in the sign that makes this sentence true.

9. Joan bought a 2,000-milliliter bottle of laundry detergent. How many liters were in the bottle of laundry detergent?

10. Which shows the use of the distributive property for $2,358 \times 2$?

11. $400 - 216 = ?$

12. If $\angle RQS$ and $\angle SQT$ are right angles, what is the value of $a + b$?

13. 30 is a multiple of 1, 2, _____, 5, _____, _____, _____, and 30.

14. Jamal is three years old. His dad is ten times older. How old is Jamal's dad?

Describe the pattern.

| | | |
|---|---|---|
| **1.**      4.OA.2<br><br>A) $14 + b = 73$<br><br>B) $73 + 14 = b$ | **2.**      4.G.1 | **3.**      4.NBT.3 |
| **4.**      4.NBT.4 | **5.**      4.NBT.1 | **6.**      4.NBT.5 |
| **7.**      4.OA.3 | **8.**      4.NF.2<br><br>$$\frac{7}{8} \bigcirc \frac{8}{8}$$ | **9.**      4.MD.1 |
| **10.**      4.NBT.5<br><br>A) $(2{,}000 \times 2) + (300 \times 2) + (500 \times 2) + (8 \times 2)$<br><br>B) $(2{,}000 \times 2) + (300 \times 2) + (50 \times 2) + (8 \times 2)$ | **11.**      4.NBT.4 | **12.**      4.MD.7 |
| **13.**      4.OA.4 | **14.**      4.OA.1 | **15.**      4.OA.5 |

# Lesson #72

1.    Find all the factor pairs for 15.

2.    If the two rays form a right angle, what is the value of *m*?

3.    Round 135,566 to the nearest hundred thousand.

4.    Monty wants to buy 32 ounces of holiday candy.  Each box is one pound.
      How many boxes will Monty have to buy?

5.    Which shows the use of the distributive property for 4,213 × 4?

6.    Which of these is a point?  Draw it in the box.   ᴄ   ●   ᴧ

7.    Fill in the numerator to show an equivalent fraction.

8.    Kennedy moved into a new house.  She had 5 boxes of items for her bedroom.
      She had 4 times as many boxes for the kitchen.  How many kitchen
      boxes were there? Write a number sentence and solve it.

9.    419,385 ◯ 419,365

10.   Use a matrix model to find the product:   63 × 36 = ?

11.   4,003 − 1,564 = ?

12.   Draw perpendicular lines.

13.   Terry Fiennes is taking a business trip.  He drives 107 miles the first day, 200
      the next day, and 111 the day after that.  After that, he drives the entire way
      home.  Did he drive more or fewer than 900 miles?

14.   389 ÷ 4 = ?

15.   Find the measure of ∠*QRS*.

| 1.        4.OA.4 | 2.        4.MD.7 | 3.        4.NBT.3 |
|---|---|---|
| | | |

| 4.        4.MD.1 | 5.        4.NBT.5 | 6.        4.G.1 |
|---|---|---|
| | A) $(4,000 \times 4) + (200 \times 4) + (0 \times 4) + (3 \times 4)$<br><br>B) $(4,000 \times 4) + (200 \times 4) + (10 \times 4) + (3 \times 4)$ | |

| 7.        4.NF.1 | 8.        4.OA.2 | 9.        4.NBT.2 |
|---|---|---|
| $\dfrac{4}{4} = \dfrac{\Box}{8}$ | | |

| 10.        4.NBT.5 | 11.        4.NBT.4 | 12.        4.G.1 |
|---|---|---|
| | | |

| 13.        4.OA.3 | 14.        4.NBT.6 | 15.        4.MD.6 |
|---|---|---|
| | | |

# Lesson #73

1.      $16,231 + 37,473 = ?$

2.      Dusty Rhodes is a traveler.  He strolls 175 miles in March, 165 miles in April, 200 miles in May, and 135 miles in June.  If he strolls 125 miles in July, will he have strolled more or fewer than 900 miles?

3.      **A fraction with a numerator of one is called a *unit fraction*.** This math sentence shows $\frac{3}{4}$ as a sum of unit fractions:  $\frac{1}{4} + \frac{1}{4} + \frac{1}{4} = \frac{3}{4}$.  Show $\frac{5}{8}$ as a sum of unit fractions.  _____ + _____ + _____ + _____ + _____ $= \frac{5}{8}$.

4.      $176 \div 4 = ?$

5.      The perimeter of this rectangle is 36 m.  The length is given.  Find the width. Remember to label your answer.

6.      $9,000 - 2,734 = ?$

7.      Describe the pattern.

8.      Write $300,000 + 60,000 + 8,000 + 50 + 2$ as a base-ten number.

9.      The parents brought 4 times as many hot dogs for the school picnic as hamburgers.  They brought 9 hamburgers.  How many hot dogs did the parents bring?

10.     Write the names of the four line segments that make up rectangle *PLUG*.

11.     Find the product of 10 and 62.  Why does the product end in a zero?

12.     Which shows the use of the distributive property for $5,013 \times 5$?

13.     Round 34,662 to the nearest ten thousand.

14.     Find the measure of $\angle HIJ$.

15.     When comparing fractions with like denominators, simply compare the numerators.  Choose the sign that makes this sentence true.

| 1.     4.NBT.4 | 2.     4.OA.3 | 3.     4.NF.3 |
|---|---|---|
| 4.     4.NBT.6 | 5.     4.MD.3<br><br>12 m<br><br>perimeter = 36 m | 6.     4.NBT.4 |
| 7.     4.OA.5 | 8.     4.NBT.2 | 9.     4.OA.1 |
| 10.     4.G.1<br><br>P       G<br>L       U | 11.     4.NBT.1 | 12.     4.NBT.5<br><br>A) $(5,000 \times 5) + (0 \times 5) + (10 \times 5) + (3 \times 5)$<br><br>B) $(5,000 \times 5) + (100 \times 5) + (10 \times 5) + (3 \times 5)$ |
| 13.     4.NBT.3 | 14.     4.MD.6 | 15.     4.NF.2<br><br>$\dfrac{5}{6} \bigcirc \dfrac{2}{6}$ |

# Lesson #74

1.  Lora scored 36 baskets in her basketball game this weekend. That was 6 times as many as she scored last weekend. Choose the best equation and use it to find out how many baskets she scored last weekend.

2.  3,762 + 8,864 = ?

3.  **One minute (min) is 60 seconds (sec).** Write *1 minute = 60 seconds* in the box.

4.  Describe the pattern.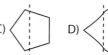

5.  Is 35 prime or composite? Explain.

6.  Which shows the use of the distributive property for 5,379 × 6?

7.  The perimeter of this rectangle is 64 m. The length is given. Find the width. Remember to label your answer.

8.  Choose the sign that makes this sentence true.

9.  493 − 187 = ?

10. Which shows a line of symmetry ?

11. Show $\dfrac{7}{10}$ as a sum of unit fractions.

    _____ + _____ + _____ + _____ + _____ + _____ + _____ = _____

12. Steven Nicks owns several music supply stores. He is ordering guitar picks. Steven always sends 125 to store one, 111 to store two, 99 to store three, and 54 to store four. He decides to double his order because his supplier is having a half-off sale. How many total guitar picks will he get?

13. Draw a pair of parallel lines in the box.

14. Is ∠LKJ acute, right, or obtuse?

15. Round 563,417 to the nearest hundred thousand.

| | | |
|---|---|---|
| **1.**    4.OA.2<br><br>A) $6 \times b = 36$<br><br>B) $36 \times 6 = b$ | **2.**    4.NBT.4 | **3.**    4.MD.1 |
| **4.**    4.OA.5 | **5.**    4.OA.4 | **6.**    4.NBT.5<br><br>A) $(5{,}000 \times 6) + (300 \times 6) + (70 \times 6) + (9 \times 6)$<br><br>B) $(5{,}000 \times 6) + (300 \times 6) + (7 \times 6) + (9 \times 6)$ |
| **7.**    4.MD.3<br>21 m<br>perimeter = 64 m | **8.**    4.NF.2<br><br>$$\frac{8}{10} \bigcirc \frac{7}{10}$$ | **9.**    4.NBT.4 |
| **10.**    4.G.3 | **11.**    4.NF.3 | **12.**    4.OA.3 |
| **13.**    4.G.1 | **14.**    4.MD.6<br><br>L   K<br>J | **15.**    4.NBT.3 |

# Lesson #75

1.  $7,000 - 1,694 = ?$

2.  During the summer, there are 5 times as many kids playing baseball as there are on the swim team. If there are 105 kids on the swim team, how many kids play baseball? Choose the correct equation and solve it.

3.  Multiplication is a way of showing repeated addition. $2 + 2 + 2 = 3 \times 2 = 6$

    Fractions can be shown the same way. $\frac{1}{2} + \frac{1}{2} + \frac{1}{2} = 3 \times \frac{1}{2} = \frac{3}{2}$ or $1\frac{1}{2}$.

    Write $\frac{1}{3} + \frac{1}{3} + \frac{1}{3} + \frac{1}{3}$ as a multiplication problem, and then find the product.

4.  List the first 5 multiples of 7.

5.  The perimeter of this rectangle is 40. The length is given. Find the width.

6.  $86 \times 92 = ?$ Complete the matrix model to find the product.

7.  Compare the unit fractions at the right. The larger the denominator, the smaller the unit is. Choose the sign that makes this sentence true.

8.  Write 45,213 in expanded form.

9.  Which lines are perpendicular?   A)  B)  C)  D)

10. $6,532 \div 4 = ?$

11. An NFL football game is one hour long. The average player plays $12\frac{1}{2}$ minutes of the game. For how many minutes of the game does the average player sit on the bench?

12. Lori finished 9 times as many math problems at home as she finished in class. In class, Lori finished 6 math problems. How many math problems did Lori finish at home?

13. Draw and label $\overline{NO}$ in the box.

14. $62,816 + 47,928 = ?$

15. Find the measure of $\angle TUV$.

| | | |
|---|---|---|
| **1.**      4.NBT.4 | **2.**      4.OA.2 <br><br> A) $k \times 5 = 105$ <br><br> B) $k = 105 \times 5$ | **3.**      4.NF.4 |
| **4.**      4.OA.4 | **5.**      4.MD.3 <br><br> 13 m <br> perimeter = 40 m | **6.**      4.NBT.5 |
| **7.**      4.NF.2 <br><br> $\dfrac{1}{6} \bigcirc \dfrac{1}{8}$ | **8.**      4.NBT.2 | **9.**      4.G.2 |
| **10.**      4.NBT.6 | **11.**      4.MD.2 | **12.**      4.OA.1 |
| **13.**      4.G.1 | **14.**      4.NBT.4 | **15.**      4.MD.6 |

# Lesson #76

1.    Round 56,347 to the nearest hundred.

2.    One minute equals _____ seconds.

3.    Find the sum.  $\frac{3}{10} + \frac{6}{10} = ?$

4.    Ellie Elwes has one month to raise $350 to pay for her sports equipment.  She decides to sell candy bars.  She raises $56 in week one, $75 in week two, and $70 in week three.  How much must she raise in week four to reach her goal?  Write an equation using $x$ to represent the amount she must make in week four.

5.    $356 \div 8 = ?$

6.    Which has parallel lines?

7.    $7,349 + 5,552 = ?$

8.    63 is a multiple of 1, 3, _____, _____, 21, and 63.

9.    The perimeter of this rectangle is 26 m.  The length is given.  Find the width.  Remember to label your answer.

10.   Choose the sign that makes this sentence true.

11.   Write $\frac{1}{5} + \frac{1}{5} + \frac{1}{5} + \frac{1}{5} + \frac{1}{5} + \frac{1}{5} + \frac{1}{5}$ as a multiplication problem, and then find the product.

12.   **Use the distributive property to multiply 41 × 25.  Use the expanded form of 41 (40 + 1) and 25 (20 + 5).  Multiply the two addends of 41 by the two addends of 25.  Then, add all the partial products to get one final product.  (40 × 20) + (40 × 5) + (1 × 20) + (1 × 5) = 800 + 200 + 20 + 5 = 1,025.**

      Use the distributive property to multiply 63 × 15.

13.   Describe the pattern.  3, 8, 13, 18, 23

14.   $5,641 - 2,265 = ?$

15.   Dogs won 7 times as many blue ribbons at the pet show as turtles won.  Turtles won 5 blue ribbons.  How many blue ribbons did dogs win?

| 1. 4.NBT.3 | 2. 4.MD.1 | 3. 4.NF.3 |
|---|---|---|
| **4.** 4.OA.3 | **5.** 4.NBT.6 | **6.** 4.G.1 |
| **7.** 4.NBT.4 | **8.** 4.OA.4 | **9.** 4.MD.3 <br><br> 8 m <br><br> perimeter = 26 m |
| **10.** 4.NF.2 <br><br> $\dfrac{5}{6} \bigcirc \dfrac{6}{6}$ | **11.** 4.NF.4 | **12.** 4.NBT.5 |
| **13.** 4.OA.5 | **14.** 4.NBT.4 | **15.** 4.OA.1 |

# Lesson #77

1. The grocery store carried 6 times as many types of cereal as types of crackers. They carried 8 types of crackers. How many types of cereal did the grocery store carry?

2. Choose the sign that makes this sentence true.

3. Write $\frac{1}{2} + \frac{1}{2} + \frac{1}{2} + \frac{1}{2} + \frac{1}{2} + \frac{1}{2}$ as a multiplication problem. Then, find the product.

4. Martino McBrood has already sold several hundred valentines for his card shop. He sold 127 on Monday, 173 on Tuesday, and 150 on Wednesday. He wants to sell as many cards Thursday as he sold on the previous three days combined. How many total cards does he hope to sell?

5. $22,656 + 39,489 = ?$

6. Use the distributive property to multiply $36 \times 12$. Use the expanded form of 36 $(30 + 6)$ and 12 $(10 + 2)$. Multiply the two addends of 36 by the two addends of 12. Then, add all the partial products to get one final product.
$(30 \times 10) + (30 \times 2) + (6 \times 10) + (6 \times 2) = 300 + 60 + 60 + 12 = 432.$

   Use the distributive property to multiply $45 \times 21$.

7. $7,364 \div 4 = ?$

8. Which lines are perpendicular?     A)   B)   C)   D)

9. If 1 minute = 60 seconds, then 2 minutes = _____ seconds.

10. Find all the factor pairs for 13.

11. $\overrightarrow{GF}$ and $\overrightarrow{GH}$ are perpendicular. What is the value of $b$?

12. Write thirty-seven thousand, nine hundred fifty-six as a base-ten number.

13. Look at the rectangle. Segments $AB$ and $BD$ run (parallel / perpendicular) to one another.

14. $9,000 - 2,774 = ?$

15. The perimeter of this rectangle is 20 mm. The width is given. Find the length. Remember to label your answer.

**1.** 4.OA.1

**2.** 4.NF.2

$$\frac{10}{12} \bigcirc \frac{8}{12}$$

**3.** 4.NF.4

**4.** 4.OA.3

**5.** 4.NBT.4

**6.** 4.NBT.5

**7.** 4.NBT.6

**8.** 4.G.2

**9.** 4.MD.1

**10.** 4.OA.4

**11.** 4.MD.7

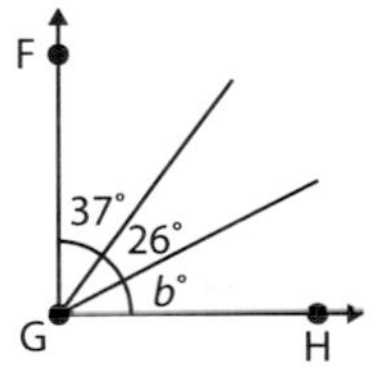
F
37°
26°
b°
G
H

**12.** 4.NBT.2

**13.** 4.G.1

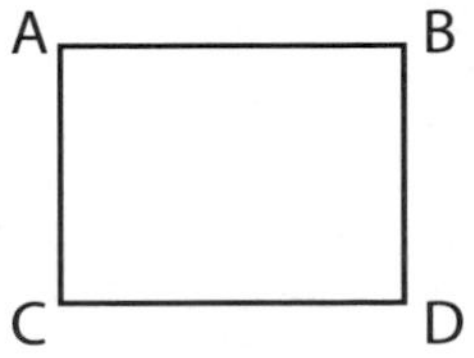
A
B
C
D

**14.** 4.NBT.4

**15.** 4.MD.3

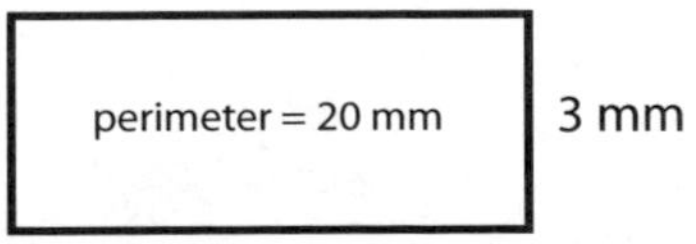
perimeter = 20 mm
3 mm

# Lesson #78

1.      3,674 + 7,816 = ?

2.      4,956 ÷ 7 = ?

3.      Write $\frac{2}{3} + \frac{2}{3} + \frac{2}{3}$ as a multiplication problem.  Then, find the product.

4.      Bernie spent 1 hour and 57 minutes knitting a scarf for her grandson.  She spent 1 hour and 21 minutes knitting a scarf for her granddaughter.  How many minutes faster did Bernie knit her granddaughter's scarf?

5.      Is 64 prime or composite?  Explain.

6.      If ∠BDF is a straight angle, what is the value of $a$?

7.      9,031 − 3,675 = ?

8.      Find the measure of ∠MLK.

9.      Use the distributive property to multiply 64 × 27.  Multiply the two addends of 64 by the two addends of 27.  Show the product.

10.     Find the sum.  $\frac{3}{10} + \frac{6}{10} = ?$

11.     Jonah's grandfather is 80 years old.  His age is 10 times Jonah's age. Choose the best equation and use it to find out how old Jonah is.

12.     Mike won the men's 1,500-meter freestyle swim event.  How many kilometers did Mike swim?

13.     Describe the pattern.   100, 91, 82, 73, 64

14.     Round 576 to the nearest hundred.

15.     Juan bought 3 times as many pencils for school this year as he bought last year.  Last year he bought 9 pencils.  How many pencils did Juan buy this year?

| 1.  4.NBT.4 | 2.  4.NBT.6 | 3.  4.NF.4 |
|---|---|---|
| 4.  4.MD.2 | 5.  4.OA.4 | 6.  4.MD.7 |
| 7.  4.NBT.4 | 8.  4.MD.6 | 9.  4.NBT.5 |
| 10.  4.NF.3 | 11.  4.OA.2<br><br>A) $10 \times j = 80$<br><br>B) $10 \times 80 = j$ | 12.  4.MD.1 |
| 13.  4.OA.5 | 14.  4.NBT.3 | 15.  4.OA.1 |

# Lesson #79

1.  Choose the sign that makes this sentence true.

2.  Find the difference. $\frac{8}{9} - \frac{3}{9} = ?$

3.  14,005 − 8,235 = ?

4.  The speedboat pulled the water skier 5.5 kilometers. How many meters did the speedboat pull the skier?

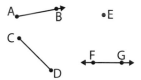

5.  In the box, write the name of each object next to its description.

6.  Elise received $10 for her birthday. She spent $5.16 on nail polish and $2.83 on lip gloss. How much did she have left?

7.  The two rays form a right angle. What is the value of $h$?

8.  Write 7,806 using words.

9.  Use the distributive property to multiply 15 × 74. Multiply the two addends of 15 (10 + 5) by the two addends of 74 (70 + 4). Show the product.

10. The perimeter of this rectangle is 32 m. The length is given. Find the width. Remember to label your answer.

11. Write $\frac{1}{4} + \frac{1}{4} + \frac{1}{4} + \frac{1}{4}$ as a multiplication problem. Then, find the product.

12. Describe the pattern. 20, 24, 28, 32, 36

13. 26,683 + 16,894 = ?

14. Paxton's baby sister weighs 7 lbs. Paxton is 7 times heavier than the baby. How much does Paxton weigh? Write a number sentence and solve it.

15. Round 416,255 to the nearest hundred thousand.

| 1.     4.NF.2 | 2.     4.NF.3 | 3.     4.NBT.4 |
|---|---|---|
| $\dfrac{4}{5} \bigcirc \dfrac{3}{5}$ | | |

| 4.     4.MD.1 | 5.     4.G.1 | 6.     4.MD.2 |
|---|---|---|
| | Line  _____  <br><br> Line Segment  _____ <br><br> Point  _____ <br><br> Ray  _____ | |

| 7.     4.MD.7 | 8.     4.NBT.2 | 9.     4.NBT.5 |
|---|---|---|
| 8°   $h°$   24° | | |

| 10.     4.MD.3 | 11.     4.NF.4 | 12.     4.OA.5 |
|---|---|---|
| 13 m <br> perimeter = 32 m | | |

| 13.     4.NBT.4 | 14.     4.OA.2 | 15.     4.NBT.3 |
|---|---|---|
| | Paxton: ? <br> Baby Sister: 7 7 7 7 7 7 7 | |

# Lesson #80

1. Which lines are parallel?

2. 62,477 + 39,586 = ?

3. The perimeter of this rectangle is 30 in. The width is given. Find the length. Remember to label your answer.

4. Round 376,415 to the nearest ten thousand.

5. 45 is a multiple of 1, _____, _____, _____, 15, and 45.

6. $\overrightarrow{AL}$ and $\overrightarrow{AZ}$ are perpendicular. What is the value of $q$?

7. Decompose (break down into smaller parts) the fraction $\frac{5}{12}$. Show this in two different ways. Here's an example: $\frac{6}{7} = \frac{5}{7} + \frac{1}{7}$ or $\frac{6}{7} = \frac{3}{7} + \frac{3}{7}$.

8. Look at the trapezoid. Which two line segments are parallel? Write their names in the box.

9. 42 × 27 = ? Complete the matrix model to find the product.

10. Violet went sledding down a 9-meter hill. She hit a patch of ice and slid 2 meters farther. How many centimeters did Violet go past the end of the hill?

11. The bug flew around for 1 minute before flying back out the window. How many seconds did the bug fly around the room?

12. 9,075 − 6,287 = ?

13. Show $\frac{2}{4}$ as a sum of unit fractions.

14. Mariana T. Wrench explores shipwrecks. On week one, she boated to a wreck 111 miles from home. On week two, she boated to a wreck 99 miles away. On week three, she boated to a wreck 150 miles away. In each case, she had to boat home as well. How many total miles did she boat?

15. Describe the pattern. 20, 18, 16, 14, 12

| | | |
|---|---|---|
| **1.**      4.G.1 | **2.**      4.NBT.4 | **3.**      4.MD.3 <br><br> perimeter = 30 in.    5 in. |
| **4.**      4.NBT.3 | **5.**      4.OA.4 | **6.**      4.MD.7 <br> L   $q°$   31°   44°   A   Z |
| **7.**      4.NF.3 | **8.**      4.G.1 <br> A    B <br> C    D | **9.**      4.NBT.5 <br> + <br> ___ + ___ |
| **10.**      4.MD.2 | **11.**      4.MD.1 | **12.**      4.NBT.4 |
| **13.**      4.NF.3 <br><br> ____ + ____ = ____ | **14.**      4.OA.3 | **15.**      4.OA.5 |

# Lesson #81

1. Which lines are perpendicular? 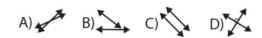 A) B) C) D)

2. Decompose the fraction $\frac{75}{100}$. Rename it in two different ways.

3. 416,310 ◯ 416,903

4. Which shows $\angle ABC$?    A)   B)   C)   D)

5. $5,000 - 1,776 = ?$

6. Mike painted 42 walls blue. That is 6 times as many as he painted red. Choose the best equation and use it to find out how many walls Mike painted red.

7. Find all the factor pairs for 16.

8. $8,375 \div 9 = ?$

9. The perimeter of this rectangle is 34 in. The length is given. Find the width. Remember to label your answer.

10. Write $\frac{3}{5} + \frac{3}{5} + \frac{3}{5} + \frac{3}{5}$ as a multiplication problem. Then, find the product.

11. Taffy Pullman just began work at a candy shop. She sells 170 caramels on Wednesday, 110 caramels on Thursday, and 90 caramels on Friday. She wants to sell 500 by the end of Saturday. What's the minimum number she must sell to reach her goal?

12. The baker made a cake that was 3 feet tall. How many yards high was the cake?

13. $23,519 + 46,882 = ?$

14. Round 4,739 to the nearest hundred.

15. Find the measure of $\angle RST$.

| 1. 4.G.2 | 2. 4.NF.3 | 3. 4.NBT.2 |
|---|---|---|
| **4.** 4.G.1 | **5.** 4.NBT.4 | **6.** 4.OA.2 <br><br> A) $42 \times 6 = p$ <br><br> B) $6 \times p = 42$ |
| **7.** 4.OA.4 | **8.** 4.NBT.6 | **9.** 4.MD.3 <br><br> perimeter = 34 in. <br><br> 11 in. |
| **10.** 4.NF.4 | **11.** 4.OA.3 | **12.** 4.MD.1 |
| **13.** 4.NBT.4 | **14.** 4.NBT.3 | **15.** 4.MD.6 <br> |

# Lesson #82

1.     $9,000 - 6,374 = ?$

2.     Is 59 prime or composite?  Explain.

3.     Find the sum.  $\frac{1}{3} + \frac{1}{3} = ?$

4.     Today, Tim walked the dogs 4 times farther than he walked them yesterday.  Yesterday he walked the dogs 2 miles.  How far did he walk the dogs today?

5.     What is the difference in length between the longest and shortest leaves in the sample?

6.     Round 64,763 to the nearest thousand.

7.     Describe the pattern.  2, 4, 9, 11, 16, 18,

8.     Jerry jumped off of the swing.  He landed 72 inches away.  How many yards did Jerry jump?

9.     Write $\frac{2}{6} + \frac{2}{6} + \frac{2}{6} + \frac{2}{6} + \frac{2}{6} + \frac{2}{6} + \frac{2}{6}$ as a multiplication problem.  Find the product.

10.     If $\angle DCB$ is a straight angle, what is the value of $x$?

11.     Tacky Tanya's Tactful Tackle Shop sells 147 worms one day, 125 the next, 163 the next, and 200 the next.  Did the shop sell more or fewer than 600 worms?

12.     Compare the unit fractions.  When comparing fractions with like numerators, remember that the larger the denominator is, the smaller the unit is.

13.     $57,886 + 83,943 = ?$

14.     Which lines are parallel?    A)    B)    C)    D)

15.     Jen's mom gave her four kids $15 to buy ice cream from the truck.  Each kid bought a cone that cost $2.25.  How much of the $15 was left?

| | | |
|---|---|---|
| **1.**      4.NBT.4 | **2.**      4.OA.4 | **3.**      4.NF.3 |
| **4.**      4.OA.1 | **5.**      4.MD.4 <br><br> **Sample Set of Leaves** (Lengths in inches) <br><br> <br> ½   1   1½   2   2½   3   3½   4   4½ | **6.**      4.NBT.3 |
| **7.**      4.OA.5 | **8.**      4.MD.1 | **9.**      4.NF.4 |
| **10.**      4.MD.7 <br><br> | **11.**      4.OA.3 | **12.**      4.NF.2 <br><br> $$\frac{1}{12} \bigcirc \frac{1}{10}$$ |
| **13.**      4.NBT.4 | **14.**      4.G.1 | **15.**      4.MD.2 |

# Lesson #83

1.      364,816 + 552,575 = ?

2.      Which lines are perpendicular?

3.      65,816 $\bigcirc$ 65,618

4.      Which shows $\angle B$?       A)        B)        C)        D)

5.      918 − 469 = ?

6.      Angie and Sterling were in different lines at the grocery store. Angie waited
        in line for 12 minutes, and Sterling waited for 9 minutes.
        How many seconds longer did Angie wait than Sterling?

7.      The cookies baked in the hot oven for 900 seconds.
        How many minutes did the cookies bake?

8.      List the first 6 multiples of 4.

9.      3,064 ÷ 8 = ?

10.     For the equation in the box, which of the following is the best estimate
        for $x$: 300, 500, or 700?

11.     When lined up end to end, what is the total length of the four shortest leaves in
        the sample?

12.     Write 21,407 in expanded form.

13.     Round 356,492 to the nearest thousand.

14.     Use the distributive property to multiply 28 × 56. Multiply the two addends of
        28 (20 + 8) by the two addends of 56 (50 + 6). Show the product.

15.     Decompose (break down into smaller parts) the mixed number $\frac{25}{12}$. Here is one
        way to show the work: $\frac{25}{12} = 1 + 1 + \frac{1}{12}$. Rename it in another way.

| | | |
|---|---|---|
| **1.**      4.NBT.4 | **2.**      4.G.2 | **3.**      4.NBT.2 |
| **4.**      4.G.1 | **5.**      4.NBT.4 | **6.**      4.MD.2 |
| **7.**      4.MD.1 | **8.**      4.OA.4 | **9.**      4.NBT.6 |
| **10.**      4.OA.3 <br><br> $235 + 265 + 104 + 98 = x$ | **11.**      4.MD.4 <br><br> **Sample Set of Leaves** (Lengths in inches) <br> | **12.**      4.NBT.2 |
| **13.**      4.NBT.3 | **14.**      4.NBT.5 | **15.**      4.NF.3 |

# Lesson #84

1. Use a protractor to draw a 90° angle. Label it ∠RTY.

2. The perimeter of this rectangle is 22 m. The width is given. Find the length. Remember to label your answer.

3. Write $\frac{3}{8} + \frac{3}{8} + \frac{3}{8} + \frac{3}{8} + \frac{3}{8}$ as a multiplication problem. Then, find the product.

4. Describe the pattern. 49, 42, 35, 28, 21

5. 456 divided by 6 = ?

6. Lori likes to take a 3,000 meter run before school. How many kilometers does Lori like to run before school?

7. 12 is a multiple of 1, _____, _____, _____, _____, and _____.

8. When lined up end to end, what is the total length of the three longest leaves in the sample?

9. 37 × 18 = ? Complete the matrix model to find the product.

10. Choose the sign that makes this sentence true.

11. Find the difference. $\frac{3}{4} - \frac{1}{4} = ?$

12. Maria sprayed 2½ liters of insecticide over her garden in May. She sprayed 450 milliliters in June and 1 liter in July. In milliliters, how much insecticide did Maria spray over her garden?

13. Which lines are parallel?

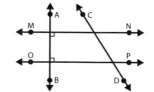

14. 36,875 − 14,589 = ?

15. 4,899 + 6,823 = ?

| | | |
|---|---|---|
| **1.** 4.MD.6 | **2.** 4.MD.3<br><br>perimeter = 22 m    4 m | **3.** 4.NF.4 |
| **4.** 4.OA.5 | **5.** 4.NBT.6 | **6.** 4.MD.1 |
| **7.** 4.OA.4 | **8.** 4.MD.4<br><br>**Sample Set of Leaves** (Lengths in inches)<br><br>½  1  1½  2  2½  3  3½  4  4½ | **9.** 4.NBT.5<br> |
| **10.** 4.NF.2<br><br>$\dfrac{78}{100} \bigcirc \dfrac{90}{100}$ | **11.** 4.NF.3 | **12.** 4.MD.2 |
| **13.** 4.G.2 | **14.** 4.NBT.4 | **15.** 4.NBT.4 |

# Lesson #85

1.      Roger is saving quarters so he can play video games at the arcade.  He wants to save $5.00 worth of quarters.  He has 6 quarters right now.  How many more quarters will Roger need to save?

2.      345,688 + 90,322 = ?

3.      Each angle is made of 2 _____ that share one _____.

4.      Use the distributive property to multiply 36 × 21.  Show the product.

5.      Room 21 has 32 books in its library.  That is 6 more than Room 19 has.  How many books does Room 19 have in its library?  Choose the correct equation and solve it.

6.      Decompose the mixed number $1\frac{3}{5}$.  Rename it in two different ways.

7.      Multiples of 2 are always even.  Multiples of 5 end in 0 or 5.  Choose the numbers that are multiples of both 2 and 5.

8.      9,703 − 3,334 = ?

9.      What is the area of this rectangle?  Label your answer.

10.     17,056 ◯ 17,506

11.     6,469 ÷ 7 = ?

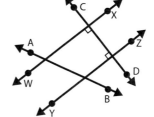

12.     Lines AB and CD are (parallel / perpendicular / neither).

13.     This year's parade had 8 times as many floats as last year's parade.  Last year there were 5 floats.  How many floats did the parade have this year?

14.     Write $\frac{1}{10} + \frac{1}{10} + \frac{1}{10} + \frac{1}{10} + \frac{1}{10} + \frac{1}{10} + \frac{1}{10} + \frac{1}{10} + \frac{1}{10} = ?$  as a multiplication problem.
        Then, find the product.

15.     One student with thumbs $1\frac{3}{4}''$ long placed his two thumbs end to end.  His friend measured the total length of the lined-up thumbs.  What was the length?

| 1. 4.MD.2 | 2. 4.NBT.4 | 3. 4.G.1 |
|---|---|---|
|  |  | |

| 4. 4.NBT.5 | 5. 4.OA.2 | 6. 4.NF.3 |
|---|---|---|
|  | A) $6 + 32 = b$  <br><br> B) $6 + b = 32$ |  |

| 7. 4.OA.4 | 8. 4.NBT.4 | 9. 4.MD.3 |
|---|---|---|
| 16   20   8   15   40 |  | |

| 10. 4.NBT.2 | 11. 4.NBT.6 | 12. 4.G.1 |
|---|---|---|
|  |  |  |

| 13. 4.OA.1 | 14. 4.NF.4 | 15. 4.MD.4 |
|---|---|---|
|  |  |  |

# Lesson #86

1.  Marta Rivera makes $107 on day one, $115 on day two, $93 on day three, and $95 on day four. If she makes about the same amount of money over the next four days, will she have made more or less than $900?

2.  Find the sum. $\frac{6}{8} + \frac{1}{8} = ?$

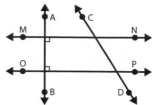

3.  $\overleftrightarrow{MN}$ and $\overleftrightarrow{OP}$ are (parallel / perpendicular / neither).

4.  Choose the number that is a multiple of 6 and 4.

5.  Draw an obtuse angle. Label it $\angle CDB$.

6.  $409 - 186 = ?$

7.  $3,677 + 9,802 = ?$

8.  Moxie the puppy was able to sit 5 minutes without moving. How many seconds was Moxie able to sit?

9.  Round 3,652 to the nearest thousand.

10. Mr. Russo made a pizza that was 2 times as wide as a small pizza. This extra large pizza had a diameter of 18 inches. What was the diameter of Mr. Russo's small pizza? Choose the correct equation and solve it.

11. What is the difference in length between the longest and the shortest thumbs in the sample?

12. When the numerators are the same, the larger the denominator, the smaller the unit is. Fill in the sign that makes this sentence true.

13. Describe the pattern.  3, 7, 10, 14, 17, 21

14. Use the fraction model to solve $4 \times \frac{2}{3}$ .

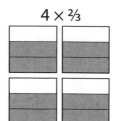

$4 \times \frac{2}{3}$

15. What is the area of a rectangle with a length of 4 m and a width of 3 m? Label the answer.

| 1.    4.OA.3 | 2.    4.NF.3 | 3.    4.G.2 |
|---|---|---|
| 4.    4.OA.4  <br><br> 18  8  16  30  12 | 5.    4.G.1 | 6.    4.NBT.4 |
| 7.    4.NBT.4 | 8.    4.MD.1 | 9.    4.NBT.3 |
| 10.    4.OA.2 <br><br> A) $p \times 2 = 18$ <br> B) $2 \times 18 = p$ | 11.    4.MD.4 <br> **Lengths of Student's Thumbs** (in.) <br> 1  1¼  1½  2  2¼  2½ | 12.    4.NF.2 <br><br> $\dfrac{4}{8} \bigcirc \dfrac{4}{10}$ |
| 13.    4.OA.5 | 14.    4.NF.4 | 15.    4.MD.3 |

# Lesson #87

1.      Write the base-ten number for 600,000 + 90,000 + 8,000 + 400 + 30 + 7.

2.      What is the area of this rectangle?  Label the answer.

3.      913 + 598 = ?

4.      Use the fraction model to solve $4 \times \frac{3}{5}$.

5.      17,804 − 8,662 = ?

6.      Constance Miles runs a tooth whitening service.  In week one, she whitens 219 teeth.  She whitens 198 in week two, and 200 in week three.  She wants to reach a goal of 900 whitened teeth for the month.  How many teeth must she whiten during the last week to meet this goal?

7.      The cinema had a movie screen that was 4 yards tall. How many feet high was the screen?

8.      5,376 divided by 8  = ?

9.      Round the number 67,034 to the nearest ten thousand.

10.     Describe the pattern.  6, 3, 9, 6, 12

11.     The two rays form a right angle.  What is the value of $z$?

12.     Draw every line of symmetry for the pentagon.  For polygons with an odd number of sides, all lines of symmetry pass through _____.

        two vertices          one vertex and one side          two sides

13.     Decompose the fraction $\frac{4}{5}$.  Rename it in two different ways.

14.     61 × 36 = ?  Complete the matrix model to find the product.

15.     Mary's thumb is $2\frac{1}{4}$".  Brad and Kevin each have $1\frac{1}{4}$" thumbs. Is Mary's thumb longer or shorter than Brad's thumb plus Kevin's? How much longer or shorter is it?

| 1.                4.NBT.2 | 2.                4.MD.3 | 3.                4.NBT.4 |
|---|---|---|
| $6,00000$ | 4 cm<br>5 cm | |

| 4.                4.NF.4 | 5.                4.NBT.4 | 6.                4.OA.3 |
|---|---|---|
| | | |

| 7.                4.MD.1 | 8.                4.NBT.6 | 9.                4.NBT.3 |
|---|---|---|
| | | |

| 10.               4.OA.5 | 11.               4.MD.7 | 12.               4.G.3 |
|---|---|---|
| | z°  32°  28° | |

| 13.               4.NF.3 | 14.               4.NBT.5 | 15.               4.MD.4 |
|---|---|---|
| | + <br> ___ + ___ | **Lengths of Student's Thumbs** (in.)<br>1  1¼  1½  2  2¼  2½ |

# Lesson #88

1. Use a protractor to draw a 30° angle. Label it ∠*PAS*.

2. 921 − 158 = ?

3. What is the difference in height between the tallest and the shortest bean stalk?

4. Round 652,355 to the nearest hundred thousand.

5. Eddy picked 5 pounds of apples from the apple tree. His mom made a pie with two pounds, 6 ounces of the apples. How many ounces of apples were left?

6. Shelby's mom put up a tent that was 72 inches tall. How many yards tall was the tent?

7. 835 ÷ 4 = ?

8. Show $\frac{4}{5}$ as a sum of unit fractions. ____ + ____ + ____ + ____ = ____

9. 4,566 + 8,725 = ?

10. $\overleftrightarrow{UV}$ and $\overleftrightarrow{WX}$ are (parallel / perpendicular / neither).

11. Choose the sign that makes this sentence true.

12. Scotty is on a budget. He is giving himself $500 to spend on clothing. He buys a jacket for $79, boots for $121, and a suit for $200. He is considering buying another suit or another jacket. Can he buy one, both, or neither?

13. Complete the fraction model to solve $6 \times \frac{3}{4}$.

14. What is the area of a rectangle with a length of 6 in. and a width of 1 in.? Label the answer.

15. $\overrightarrow{XW}$ and $\overrightarrow{XY}$ are perpendicular. What is the value of *d*?

| 1.    4.MD.6 | 2.    4.NBT.4 | 3.    4.MD.4 |
|---|---|---|
| | | **Heights of Bean Stalks** (inches) 1½   2   2½   3   3½   4   4½   5   5½ |
| 4.    4.NBT.3 | 5.    4.MD.2 | 6.    4.MD.1 |
| | | |
| 7.    4.NBT.6 | 8.    4.NF.3 | 9.    4.NBT.4 |
| | | |
| 10.    4.G.1 | 11.    4.NF.2 $$\frac{9}{10} \bigcirc \frac{7}{10}$$ | 12.    4.OA.3 Add the compatible numbers, then you can use mental math! |
| 13.    4.NF.4 | 14.    4.MD.3 | 15.    4.MD.7 |

# Lesson #89

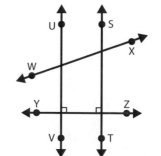

1.  $609 + 388 = ?$

2.  $\overrightarrow{YZ}$ and $\overleftrightarrow{ST}$ are (parallel / perpendicular / neither).

3.  Use words to write 3,472.

4.  $597 \div 5 = ?$

5.  Decompose the mixed number $3\frac{3}{6}$. Rename it in two different ways.

6.  If $\angle BAC$ and $\angle CAD$ are right angles, what is the value of $x$?

7.  Molly beat Trish in the race by 120 seconds. By how many minutes did Molly beat Trish?

8.  Abi called Ella 3 times more than she called Mia. She called Mia 6 times. How many times did Abi call Ella?

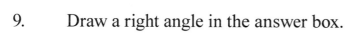

9.  Draw a right angle in the answer box.

10. $4,000 - 2,368 = ?$

11. List the first 7 multiples of 3.

12. Complete the fraction model to solve $5 \times \frac{2}{6}$.

13. Add the height of the tallest plant with the height of one of the next tallest plants. What is the total height?

14. What is the area of a rectangle with a length of 5 mm and a width of 3 mm? Label the answer.

15. Use the distributive property to multiply $17 \times 58$. Show the product.

**1.** 4.NBT.4

**2.** 4.G.1

**3.** 4.NBT.2

**4.** 4.NBT.6

**5.** 4.NF.3

**6.** 4.MD.7

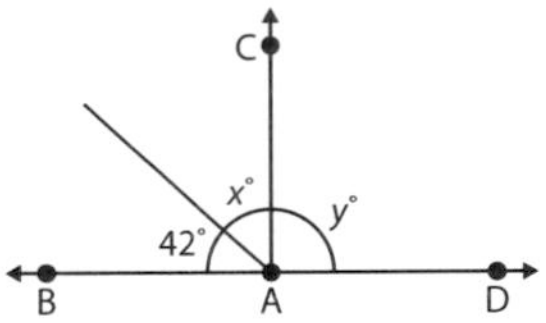
C
x°
y°
42°
B
A
D

**7.** 4.MD.1

**8.** 4.OA.1

**9.** 4.G.1

**10.** 4.NBT.4

**11.** 4.OA.4

**12.** 4.NF.4

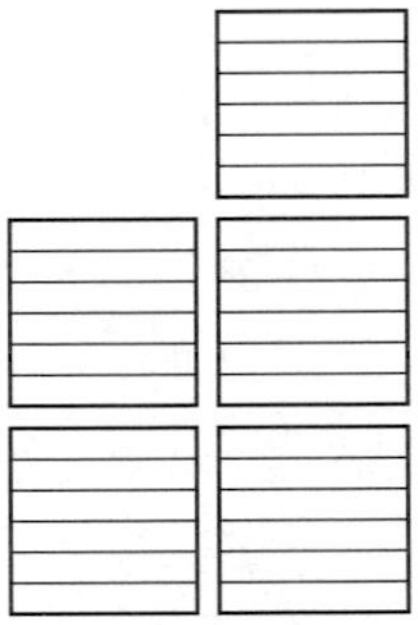

**13.** 4.MD.4

**Heights of Bean Stalks** (inches)

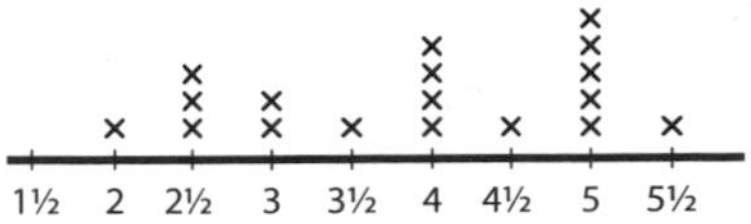
1½ 2 2½ 3 3½ 4 4½ 5 5½

**14.** 4.MD.3

**15.** 4.NBT.5

# Lesson #90

1. To compare fractions with like numerators, remember that the larger the denominator is, the smaller the unit is. Choose the sign that makes this sentence true.

2. Tessa went to the mall with $23.40. She came home with $5.93. How much money did Tessa spend at the mall?

3. $168,247 + 249,813 = ?$

4. What is the area of this rectangle? Label the answer.

5. Find the sum. $\dfrac{2}{6} + \dfrac{2}{6} = ?$

6. Roscoe is throwing balls at a tower of milk bottles at the fair. Each throw costs 5 tokens. Roscoe has 43 tokens. How many times can Roscoe throw the ball?

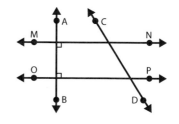

7. The kitten weighed 1 kilogram. How many grams did the kitten weigh?

8. $3,000 - 988 = ?$

9. 64 is a multiple of 1, 2, _____, _____, 16, _____, and 64.

10. $58 \times 29 = ?$ Complete the matrix model to find the product.

11. $6,056 \div 4 = ?$

12. $\overleftrightarrow{MN}$ and $\overleftrightarrow{OP}$ are (parallel / perpendicular / neither).

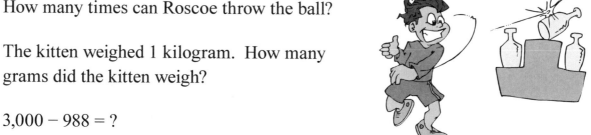

13. Describe the pattern. 1, 3, 4, 6, 7, 9, 10, 12

14. Find the sum. Remember to rename fractions that have a numerator that is larger than the denominator. Write the sum as a mixed number.

$$\frac{2}{4} + \frac{3}{4} = \frac{5}{4} \qquad \frac{5}{4} = \frac{4}{4} + \frac{\Box}{\Box} = ?$$

15. Round 516,833 to the nearest thousand.

| | | |
|---|---|---|
| **1.**  4.NF.2 $$\frac{3}{3} \bigcirc \frac{3}{5}$$ | **2.**  4.MD.2 | **3.**  4.NBT.4 |
| **4.**  4.MD.3<br>4 mm<br>9 mm | **5.**  4.NF.3 | **6.**  4.OA.3 |
| **7.**  4.MD.1 | **8.**  4.NBT.4 | **9.**  4.OA.4 |
| **10.**  4.NBT.5 | **11.**  4.NBT.6 | **12.**  4.G.1 |
| **13.**  4.OA.5 | **14.**  4.NF.3 $$\frac{4}{4} + \frac{\square}{\square} = \underline{\qquad}$$ | **15.**  4.NBT.3 |

# Lesson #91

1. The band will play for 60 minutes. If the members want to play 5 songs of equal length, how many seconds will each song have to be?

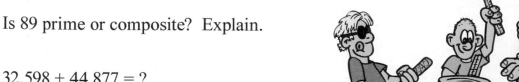

2. Is 89 prime or composite? Explain.

3. $32,598 + 44,877 = ?$

4. $314 - 87 = ?$

5. Complete the fraction model to solve $3 \times \frac{2}{4}$.

6. $146,207 \bigcirc 146,027$

7. Natalie is reading 7 pages a day in her science book. She has 58 pages to read. How many days will it take her to finish them?

8. Decompose the fraction $\frac{7}{8}$. Rename it in two different ways.

9. If 1 liter = 1,000 mL, then 3 liters = _____ mL.

10. If you stacked the two tallest blocks on top of one another, what total height would you measure?

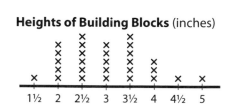

**Heights of Building Blocks** (inches)

11. Round 486,975 to the nearest ten thousand.

12. Use the distributive property to multiply $43 \times 20$. Show the product.

13. Use a protractor to draw a 110° angle. Label it $\angle LZX$.

14. $2,082 \div 4 = ?$

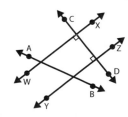

15. Lines *WX* and *YZ* are (parallel / perpendicular / neither).

| | | |
|---|---|---|
| **1.** 4.MD.2 | **2.** 4.OA.4 | **3.** 4.NBT.4 |
| **4.** 4.NBT.4 | **5.** 4.NF.4 | **6.** 4.NBT.2 |
| **7.** 4.OA.3 | **8.** 4.NF.3 | **9.** 4.MD.1 |
| **10.** 4.MD.4 | **11.** 4.NBT.3 | **12.** 4.NBT.5 |
| **13.** 4.MD.6 | **14.** 4.NBT.6 | **15.** 4.G.1 |

# Lesson #92

1.  The snow was 54 inches deep.  How many feet deep was the snow?

2.  Choose the sign that makes this sentence true.

3.  $4,658 + 8,807 = ?$

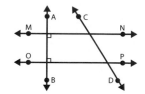

4.  $\overrightarrow{AB}$ and $\overrightarrow{OP}$ are (parallel / perpendicular / neither).

5.  Complete the fraction model to solve $6 \times \dfrac{4}{5}$.

6.  $94 \times 43 = ?$
    Complete the matrix model to find the product.

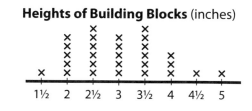

7.  $4,000 - 2,344 = ?$

8.  What is the area of a rectangle with a length of 8 cm and a width of 7 cm?
    Label the answer.

9.  What is the difference in height between the tallest and shortest block?

**Heights of Building Blocks** (inches)

10. $234 \div 3 = ?$

11. Describe the pattern.  4, 2, 6, 4, 8, 6, 10

12. Round 3,785 to the nearest hundred.

13. The bakery is displaying cupcakes on 8 shelves.  How many cupcakes will go on each shelf if there are 75 cupcakes?

14. The two rays form a right angle.  What is the value of $g$?

15. Find the difference.  $\dfrac{5}{8} - \dfrac{2}{8} = ?$

| | | |
|---|---|---|
| **1.** 4.MD.1 | **2.** 4.NF.2 $$\frac{5}{6} \bigcirc \frac{2}{6}$$ | **3.** 4.NBT.4 |
| **4.** 4.G.1 | **5.** 4.NF.4 | **6.** 4.NBT.5 |
| **7.** 4.NBT.4 | **8.** 4.MD.3 | **9.** 4.MD.4 |
| **10.** 4.NBT.6 | **11.** 4.OA.5 | **12.** 4.NBT.3 |
| **13.** 4.OA.3 | **14.** 4.MD.7 | **15.** 4.NF.3 |

# Lesson #93

1. Write $200,000 + 40,000 + 600 + 20 + 2$ as a base-ten number.

2. Derek and Josh decided to build a tower of blocks. Before lunch, Derek built $\frac{3}{8}$ of the tower. Josh built $\frac{4}{8}$ of the tower. How much of the tower did the boys complete before lunch?

3. Tracy's cat was stuck high in a tree. She had climbed 750 centimeters. How many meters high was the cat?

4. $6,000 - 4,976 = ?$

5. Can D'Angelo build a tower at least 4″ tall by stacking three $1\frac{1}{2}$″ blocks?

6. $56,907 + 23,455 = ?$

7. Describe the pattern.  3, 10, 17, 24, 31
   Are the numbers always even, always odd, or do they alternate?

8. Draw every line of symmetry for the hexagon. For polygons with an even number of sides, all lines of symmetry pass through either _____. (pick two)

    two vertices          one vertex and one side          two sides

9. Write the sum as a mixed number.  $\dfrac{3}{4} + \dfrac{3}{4} = \dfrac{6}{4} \rightarrow \dfrac{6}{4} = \dfrac{4}{4} + \dfrac{\Box}{\Box} = ?$

10. Choose the multiples of 2.          4     35     22     7     40

11. Use a protractor to draw a 15° angle. Label it $\angle CVB$.

12. Bella went to the local fair with $6.00. She came home with $2.19. How much money did Bella spend at the fair?

13. $9,325 \div 5 = ?$

14. What is the area of this rectangle? Label the answer.

15. Decompose the mixed number $2\frac{4}{10}$. Rename it in two different ways.

| 1. 4.NBT.2 | 2. 4.NF.3 | 3. 4.MD.1 |
|---|---|---|
| 4. 4.NBT.4 | 5. 4.MD.2 | 6. 4.NBT.4 |
| 7. 4.OA.5 | 8. 4.G.3 | 9. 4.NF.3 |
| 10. 4.OA.4 | 11. 4.MD.6 | 12. 4.MD.2 |
| 13. 4.NBT.6 | 14. 4.MD.3 | 15. 4.NF.3 |

# Lesson #94

1. The library wants to display books on 6 shelves. They have 38 books to shelve. How many books will they be able to put on each shelf to display all the books?

2. What do you get when you add the height of two of the tallest saplings?

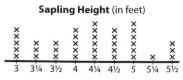

**Sapling Height** (in feet)

3. The barber had 7 times as many short hair cuts as long hair cuts. He had 5 long hair cuts. How many short hair cuts did the barber have?

4. $4,569 + 9,802 = ?$

5. Choose the sign that makes this sentence true.

6. $2,615 \div 9 = ?$

7. Write 6,849 in words.

8. Decompose the fraction $\frac{10}{100}$. Rename it in two different ways.

9. Use a protractor to draw a 105° angle. Label it $\angle NMQ$.

10. Lines $\overleftrightarrow{UV}$ and $\overleftrightarrow{YZ}$ are (parallel / perpendicular / neither).

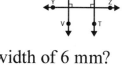

11. What is the area of a rectangle with a length of 8 mm and a width of 6 mm? Label the answer.

12. Write the name of the right angle in the answer box.

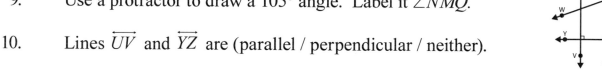

$\angle ABC$        $\angle DEF$        $\angle GHI$        $\angle JKL$

13. $54,005 - 39,763 = ?$

14. Use the distributive property to multiply $34 \times 54$. Show the product.

15. Jennifer and Christian were writing a song for music class. For homework Jennifer wrote $\frac{3}{10}$ of the song, and Christian wrote $\frac{2}{10}$ of the song. How much of the song was done when they went to class?

| 1.      4.OA.3 | 2.      4.MD.4 | 3.      4.OA.1 |
|---|---|---|
| 4.      4.NBT.4 | 5.      4.NF.2 $$\frac{5}{8} \bigcirc \frac{5}{6}$$ | 6.      4.NBT.6 |
| 7.      4.NBT.2 | 8.      4.NF.3 | 9.      4.MD.6 |
| 10.      4.G.1 | 11.      4.MD.3 | 12.      4.G.1 |
| 13.      4.NBT.4 | 14.      4.NBT.5 | 15.      4.NF.3 |

# Lesson #95

1.  Decompose the fraction $\frac{5}{12}$. Rename it in two different ways.

2.  An ice cream truck sells 55 popsicles per day in July. That is 11 times as many as in September. How many popsicles does the truck sell in September? Write an equation with $x$ as the unknown and solve it.

3.  Lines $\overrightarrow{AB}$ and $\overrightarrow{ZY}$ are (parallel / perpendicular / neither).

    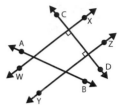

4.  Round 25,679 to the nearest ten thousand.

5.  Complete the fraction model to solve $5 \times \frac{2}{4}$.

6.  $\overrightarrow{GJ}$ and $\overrightarrow{GK}$ are perpendicular. What is the value of $e$?

7.  $28,593 + 90,442 = ?$

8.  $512 - 233 = ?$

9.  Find all the factor pairs for 18.

10. What is the difference in height between the tallest sapling and the shortest sapling?

    **Sapling Height** (in feet)

    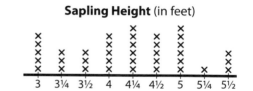

11. $61 \times 36 = ?$ Complete the matrix model to find the product.

12. Which two lines are parallel?

13. The watch repairman needs to replace the battery on some watches. He has 43 minutes before closing. How many batteries can he replace if each replacement takes 8 minutes and how many minutes will be left over?

14. Write 423,866 in expanded form.

15. What is the area of this rectangle? Label the answer.

| | | |
|---|---|---|
| **1.**　　　4.NF.3 | **2.**　　　4.OA.2 | **3.**　　　4.G.1 |
| **4.**　　　4.NBT.3 | **5.**　　　4.NF.4 | **6.**　　　4.MD.7 |
| **7.**　　　4.NBT.4 | **8.**　　　4.NBT.4 | **9.**　　　4.OA.4 |
| **10.**　　　4.MD.4 | **11.**　　　4.NBT.5 | **12.**　　　4.G.1 |
| **13.**　　　4.OA.3 | **14.**　　　4.NBT.2 | **15.**　　　4.MD.3 |

# Lesson #96

1. Show $\frac{5}{10}$ as the sum of unit fractions. ___ + ___ + ___ + ___ + ___ = ___

2. If $\angle MNO$ is a straight angle, what is the value of $y$?

3. Find all the factor pairs for 27.

4. $7,000 - 3,885 = ?$

5. $\overleftrightarrow{DC}$ and $\overrightarrow{XW}$ are (parallel / perpendicular / neither).

6. Choose the sign that makes this sentence true.

7. Sparky Lerman owns a fireworks store. He sells sparklers in boxes of 35 and boxes of 75. One customer buys four boxes of each. About how many sparklers did Sparky Lerman sell in all, 300, 400, or 500?

8. $5,677 + 8,882 = ?$

9. What is the area of a rectangle with a length of 11 in. and a width of 8 in.? Label the answer.

10. Replace the mixed number with an equivalent fraction. Then, subtract. $1\frac{2}{8} - \frac{4}{8} \rightarrow 1\frac{2}{8} = \frac{8}{8} + \frac{2}{8} = \frac{10}{8}$ so, $\frac{10}{8} - \frac{4}{8} = ?$

11. Pete swam 6 feet before taking a breath. How many yards did Pete swim?

12. Scott eats $\frac{5}{8}$ of a bag of baby carrots each week. How many bags of baby carrots does Scott eat in 4 weeks? Between what two whole numbers does your answer lie?

13. $45,632 \bigcirc 45,326$

14. If the three tallest saplings are laid end to end, what total length would they measure?

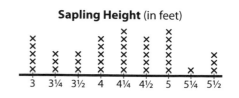

Sapling Height (in feet)

15. Round 4,766 to the nearest thousand.

| | | |
|---|---|---|
| **1.**  4.NF.3 | **2.**  4.MD.7 | **3.**  4.OA.4 |
| | | |
| **4.**  4.NBT.4 | **5.**  4.G.1 | **6.**  4.NF.2 |
| | | $\dfrac{6}{12} \bigcirc \dfrac{8}{12}$ |
| **7.**  4.OA.3 | **8.**  4.NBT.4 | **9.**  4.MD.3 |
| | | |
| **10.**  4.NF.3 | **11.**  4.MD.1 | **12.**  4.NF.4 |
| | | |
| **13.**  4.NBT.2 | **14.**  4.MD.4 | **15.**  4.NBT.3 |
| | | |

# Lesson #97

1. Round 437,816 to the nearest ten thousand.

2. $31,245 + 68,762 = ?$

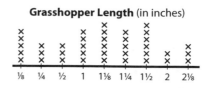

**Grasshopper Length** (in inches)

⅛   ¼   ½   1   1⅛   1¼   1½   2   2⅛

3. What is the difference in length between the longest of grasshoppers and the shortest?

4. Paul's parents drove home from vacation. On Saturday, Paul's mom drove $\frac{5}{12}$ of the trip, and Paul's dad drove $\frac{3}{12}$ of the trip. How much of the drive did Paul's parents complete on Saturday?

5. The talent show lasts for 45 minutes. How many 6-minute acts will they be able to have in the show?

6. $350 \div 6 = ?$

7. Kiren untangled the jump ropes for camp. She put them end to end and they measured 108 inches long. How many yards of jump ropes were there?

8. Lorenzo's bean plant grew $\frac{6}{10}$ of an inch every day. How tall was Lorenzo's bean plant after 7 days? Between what two whole numbers does you answer lie?

9. Use the distributive property to multiply $45 \times 71$. Show the product.

10. What is the area of this rectangle? Label the answer.

11. $641 - 298 = ?$

12. Decompose the mixed number $4\frac{2}{100}$. Rename it in two different ways.

13. An African Elephant will grow to about 12 feet tall. That is 4 times as tall as when it was born. How tall is a baby African Elephant when it is born? Write an equation with $x$ as the unknown and solve it.

14. Which shape has parallel sides?   A)    B)    C)    D)

15. Write 476,238 in expanded form.

| 1.      4.NBT.3 | 2.      4.NBT.4 | 3.      4.MD.4 |
|---|---|---|
| 4.      4.NF.3 | 5.      4.OA.3 | 6.      4.NBT.6 |
| 7.      4.MD.1 | 8.      4.NF.4 | 9.      4.NBT.5 |
| 10.      4.MD.3<br><br>8 cm<br>4 cm | 11.      4.NBT.4 | 12.      4.NF.3 |
| 13.      4.OA.2 | 14.      4.G.2 | 15.      4.NBT.2 |

# Lesson #98

1. Describe the pattern.  5, 11, 17, 23, 29
   Are the numbers always even, always odd, or do they alternate?

2. $766 \div 2 = ?$

3. Tony was so tired that he fell fast asleep in 4.5 minutes.
   How many seconds did it take Tony to fall asleep?

4. Use the fraction model to solve $6 \times \dfrac{2}{3}$.

5. What length do you get by measuring all of the
   shortest grasshoppers end-to-end?

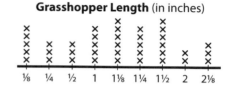

6. Round 167,419 to the nearest ten thousand.

7. $396 + 119 = ?$

8. When Alex went hiking, his backpack weighed 24 pounds.  That was 6 times
   as heavy as his empty backpack.  How much did the empty backpack weigh?
   Write an equation with $n$ as the unknown and solve it.

9. What is the area of a rectangle with a length of 9 cm and a width of 8 cm?
   Label the answer.

10. When the clock shows one o'clock, the hands form a 30° angle.  What angle do
    the arms form when the clock shows five o'clock?

11. Find the difference.  $\dfrac{50}{100} - \dfrac{25}{100} = ?$

12. Choose the sign that makes this sentence true.

13. Which shape has perpendicular sides?  Circle it.

14. $37 \times 35 = ?$  Complete the matrix model to find the product.

15. Mary Beth uses $\dfrac{7}{12}$ yards of fabric to make a pillow.  If she is making pillows
    for 3 friends, how much fabric will she use?  Between what two whole numbers
    does your answer lie?

| | | |
|---|---|---|
| **1.**     4.OA.5 | **2.**     4.NBT.6 | **3.**     4.MD.1 |
| **4.**     4.NF.4 | **5.**     4.MD.4 | **6.**     4.NBT.3 |
| **7.**     4.NBT.4 | **8.**     4.OA.2 | **9.**     4.MD.3 |
| **10.**     4.MD.7 | **11.**     4.NF.3 | **12.**     4.NF.2 $\frac{3}{5} \bigcirc \frac{3}{6}$ |
| **13.**     4.G.2 | **14.**     4.NBT.5 | **15.**     4.NF.4 |

# Lesson #99

1.    Decompose the fraction $\frac{3}{4}$. Rename it in two different ways.

2.    Use the distributive property to multiply 7,338 × 7. Show the product.

3.    The two rays form a right angle. What is the value of *s*?

4.    8,496 + 7,562 = ?

5.    Carrie had $1\frac{1}{2}$ liters of paint left in a can. She bought 3 more liters. Altogether, how many milliliters of paint did Carrie have?

6.    Which is an acute angle?     A) ⌐→     B) ↘→     C) ◺⇄     D) ↢⌣→

7.    Write *four thousand, six hundred fifty* as a base-ten number.

8.    Danny answered 36 trivia questions correctly. That was 4 times as many as his brother, Kevin, answered correctly. How many questions did Kevin answer correctly? Write an equation with *n* as the unknown and solve it.

9.    9,000 − 3,664 = ?

10.   Round 364,219 to the nearest hundred thousand.

11.   What is the sum when you add the length of one of the second longest grasshoppers to the length of one of the longest grasshoppers?

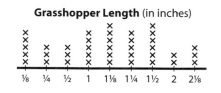

**Grasshopper Length** (in inches)

⅛    ¼    ½    1    1⅛    1¼    1½    2    2⅛

12.   Find the sum. Remember to rename fractions that have a numerator that is larger than the denominator. Write the sum as a mixed number.

$$\frac{6}{10}+\frac{7}{10}=\frac{13}{10}\rightarrow\frac{13}{10}=\frac{10}{10}+\frac{\square}{\square}=?$$

13.   358 ÷ 4 = ?

14.   What is the area of this rectangle? Label the answer.

15.   Kevin's dog Rufus eats $\frac{1}{2}$ cup of dog food each day. How much dog food will Rufus eat in 9 days? Between what two numbers does your answer lie?

| | | |
|---|---|---|
| **1.**       4.NF.3 | **2.**       4.NBT.5 | **3.**       4.MD.7 |
| **4.**       4.NBT.4 | **5.**       4.MD.2 | **6.**       4.G.1 |
| **7.**       4.NBT.2 | **8.**       4.OA.2 | **9.**       4.NBT.4 |
| **10.**       4.NBT.3 | **11.**       4.MD.4 | **12.**       4.NF.3 $$\frac{10}{10} + \frac{\square}{\square} = \underline{\hspace{1cm}}$$ |
| **13.**       4.NBT.6 | **14.**       4.MD.3 7 in. / 9 in. | **15.**       4.NF.4 |

# Lesson #100

1.   $34{,}719 + 26{,}875 = ?$

2.   Chef Jeremy uses $\frac{2}{3}$ cup of cake batter to make one mini-cake.  He is making 3 cakes, one for each of his triplet nephews.  How much cake batter will he use?  Is the answer greater or less than 3?

3.   Les S. More is an art critic.  He travels 60 miles to one art show, 25 miles to another, 140 miles to another, and 75 to another.  Each time he goes, he drives the same distance home.  Does he drive more or fewer than 500 miles in all?

4.   Choose the sign that makes this sentence true.

5.   Which shape has parallel sides?          A)◯    B)⬠    C)◺    D)▱

6.   Write $6{,}000 + 500 + 8$ as a base-ten number.

7.   Show $\frac{2}{3}$ as the sum of unit fractions.  ____ + ____ = ____

8.   Farmer Phil sold his corn at the market.  The first day he sold $\frac{3}{8}$ of his harvest.  The second day he sold $\frac{4}{8}$ of his harvest.  During the two days at the market, how much of his corn harvest did he sell?

9.   $712 - 366 = ?$

10.  What is the difference in length between the longest fish measured and the second shortest fish?

11.  What is the area of a rectangle with a length of 6 m and a width of 9 m?  Label the answer.

12.  Read the table in the box.  Fill in the missing values.

13.  **To add fractions, the denominators must be the same.  Express (show) a fraction with a denominator of 10 as an equivalent fraction with a denominator of 100.  One tenth is equal to ten hundredths.**

  $\frac{1}{10} = \frac{10}{100}$     $\frac{6}{10} + \frac{2}{100} = \frac{60}{100} + \frac{2}{100} = \frac{62}{100}$     Find the sum.  $\frac{2}{10} + \frac{6}{100} =$ ____

14.  Use a protractor to draw a 150° angle.  Label it $\angle TYU$.

15.  $4{,}242 \div 3 = ?$

**1.** 4.NBT.4

**2.** 4.NF.4

**3.** 4.OA.3

**4.** 4.NF.2

$$\frac{7}{12} \bigcirc \frac{5}{12}$$

**5.** 4.G.2

**6.** 4.NBT.2

**7.** 4.NF.3

**8.** 4.NF.3

**9.** 4.NBT.4

**10.** 4.MD.4

**Fish Length** (in inches)

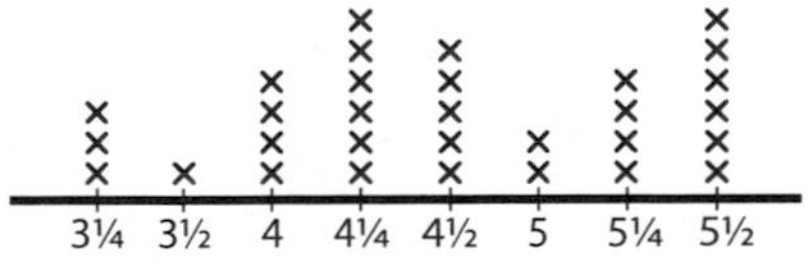
3¼
3½
4
4¼
4½
5
5¼
5½

**11.** 4.MD.3

**12.** 4.MD.1

| km | m |
|---|---|
| 1 | 1,000 |
| 2 | |
| 3 | |

**13.** 4.NF.5

**14.** 4.MD.6

**15.** 4.NBT.6

# Lesson #101

1. Find the sum. $\frac{8}{10} + \frac{9}{100} = ?$ Change tenths to hundredths before you add.

2. Round 476,215 to the nearest ten thousand.

3. What is the area of this rectangle? Label the answer.

4. Use the fraction model to solve $5 \times \frac{3}{5}$.

5. Describe the pattern. 3, 6, 9, 12, 15 Are the numbers always even, always odd, or do they alternate?

6. Decompose the mixed number $2\frac{3}{5}$. Rename it in two different ways.

7. Which shows the use of the distributive property for $12 \times 76$?

8. $86,214 + 38,455 = ?$

9. $\overrightarrow{DC}$ and $\overrightarrow{DB}$ are perpendicular. What is the value of $u$?

10. Which shape has perpendicular sides?   A)  B)  C) D)

11. $7,000 - 2,556 = ?$

12. 7,855 divided by 9 = ?

13. The toy company is making toy fire engines. Each fire engine needs 8 wheels. How many fire engines can the toy company make if they have 74 wheels?

14. If you placed one of the second longest and one of the shortest fish end-to-end, what would be the total length?

15. Mario's Pizza Shop uses $\frac{7}{8}$ pound of pepperoni each day. How much pepperoni does the pizza shop use in 5 days? Between what two whole numbers does your answer lie?

**1.**      4.NF.5

**2.**      4.NBT.3

**3.**      4.MD.3

9 mm

5 mm

**4.**      4.NF.4

**5.**      4.OA.5

**6.**      4.NF.3

**7.**      4.NBT.5

A) $(10 \times 70) + (10 \times 6) + (2 \times 70) + (2 \times 6)$

B) $(10 \times 70) + (10 \times 6) + (20 \times 70) + (2 \times 6)$

**8.**      4.NBT.4

**9.**      4.MD.7

C

53°

u°

21°

D      B

**10.**      4.G.2

**11.**      4.NBT.4

**12.**      4.NBT.6

**13.**      4.OA.3

**14.**      4.MD.4

**Fish Length** (in inches)

X
X   X   X
X   X   X   X     X
X    X   X   X   X   X   X
X    X   X   X   X   X   X   X

3¼   3½   4   4¼   4½   5   5¼   5½

**15.**      4.NF.4

# Lesson #102

1.   Which shape has perpendicular sides?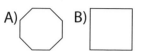

2.   Write 6,409 using words.

3.   Write the sum as a mixed number.     $\dfrac{7}{12} + \dfrac{6}{12} = \dfrac{13}{12} \rightarrow \dfrac{13}{12} = \dfrac{12}{12} + \dfrac{\square}{\square} = ?$

4.   What is the area of a rectangle with a length of 4 m and a width of 3 m? Label the answer.

5.   Tony made a cake.  The cake had 1 kg of white cake mix, 195 g of sprinkles, 450 g of whipped topping, and 670 g of mini candies.  How many grams of ingredients were used?

6.   Round 325,206 to the nearest hundred thousand.

7.   $903 - 266 = ?$

8.   If Mrs. Parsons gave each of the 6 children in her reading group $\dfrac{1}{5}$ package of crackers, how many packages of crackers would she need?  Between which two whole numbers does your answer lie?

9.   $14,244 + 26,376 = ?$

10.  Use an equivalent fraction to find the sum of $\dfrac{2}{10} + \dfrac{54}{100}$.

11.  $4,625 \div 5 = ?$

12.  What is the difference in height between the tallest of primates recorded on the line plot and the shortest primates recorded?

13.  Show $\dfrac{4}{8}$ as the sum of unit fractions.      ____ + ____ + ____ + ____ = ____

14.  $52 \times 35 = ?$   Complete the matrix model to find the product.

15.  Choose the sign that makes this sentence true.

| | | |
|---|---|---|
| **1.** 4.G.2 | **2.** 4.NBT.2 | **3.** 4.NF.3 |
| **4.** 4.MD.3 | **5.** 4.MD.2 | **6.** 4.NBT.3 |
| **7.** 4.NBT.4 | **8.** 4.NF.4 | **9.** 4.NBT.4 |
| **10.** 4.NF.5 | **11.** 4.NBT.6 | **12.** 4.MD.4 |

**12.** 4.MD.4

**Primate Height** (in feet)

| Lemurs | Long-Nosed Monkey | Chimpanzees |

**13.** 4.NF.3

**14.** 4.NBT.5

**15.** 4.NF.2

$$\frac{12}{12} \bigcirc \frac{11}{12}$$

# Lesson #103

1. Read the table.  Fill in the missing values.

2. $63,214 + 78,567 = ?$

3. If $\angle XYZ$ is a straight angle, what is the value of $b$?

4. Choose the numbers that are multiples of both 2 and 9.

5. Which triangle shows all acute angles?   A) B) C) D)

6. Round 137,541 to the nearest ten thousand.

7. What is the area of a rectangle with a length of 6 in. and a width of 7 in.?
   Label the answer.

8. What is the difference in height between the tallest lemurs and the shortest
   chimpanzees?

9. $703 - 266 = ?$

10. Decompose the fraction $\frac{5}{6}$.  Rename it in two different ways.

11. Dylan's grandmother is making lemon cookies for the bake sale.  The recipe
    calls for 5 cups of sugar.  She has 28 cups of sugar on hand.  How many batches
    of lemon cookies can Dylan's grandmother make for the bake sale?

12. Zack eats $\frac{4}{6}$ of a bag of sunflower seeds during each of his baseball games.
    How many bags of sunflower seeds will he need for his 7-game season?
    Between what two numbers does your answer lie?

13. At the hot air balloon festival, $\frac{3}{10}$ of the balloons were red, $\frac{5}{10}$ were blue,
    and $\frac{2}{10}$ were green.  What fraction of the balloons were <u>not</u> green?

14. Write 35,412 in expanded form.

15. Which shows the use of the distributive property for $27 \times 64$?

**1.**        4.MD.1

| kg | g |
|----|-------|
| 1  | 1,000 |
| 2  |       |
| 3  |       |

**2.**        4.NBT.4

**3.**        4.MD.7

77°  37°  $b°$

X     Y     Z

**4.**        4.OA.4

9    12    21    18    36

**5.**        4.G.1

**6.**        4.NBT.3

**7.**        4.MD.3

**8.**        4.MD.4

**Primate Height** (in feet)

×
×                 ×     ×
×    ×            ×    ×    ×
×    ×    ×    ×    ×    ×    ×
×    ×               ×    ×    ×

1   1½   2   2½   3   3½   4

Lemurs    Long-Nosed Monkey    Chimpanzees

**9.**        4.NBT.4

**10.**        4.NF.3

**11.**        4.OA.3

**12.**        4.NF.4

**13.**        4.NF.3

**14.**        4.NBT.2

**15.**        4.NBT.5

A) $(20 \times 60) + (20 \times 4) + (7 \times 60) + (7 \times 4)$

B) $(20 \times 6) + (20 \times 4) + (7 \times 60) + (7 \times 4)$

# Lesson #104

1.  Write the base-ten number for $50,000 + 4,000 + 600 + 20 + 3$.

2.  Find the sum. $\dfrac{1}{4} + \dfrac{2}{4} = ?$

3.  If the shortest chimpanzee stood on the tallest lemur's head, what would the total height be?

4.  $974,274 - 264,502 = ?$

5.  Michael swims $\dfrac{3}{5}$ a mile every day as part of his exercise routine. How many miles will he swim over the next 8 days? Between what two numbers does your answer lie?

6.  Read the table. Fill in the missing values.

7.  The school hosted a spaghetti dinner. There are only 25 meatballs left. Each spaghetti dinner gets 3 meatballs. How many more spaghetti dinners can the school serve and how many meatballs will be left over?

8.  Round 57,364 to the nearest ten thousand.

9.  Fill in the sign that makes this sentence true.

10. Use an equivalent fraction to find the sum of $\dfrac{4}{10} + \dfrac{8}{100}$.

11. Which shows the use of the distributive property for $33 \times 57$?

12. What is the area of this rectangle? Label the answer.

13. $1,645 \div 7 = ?$

14. Which shape has parallel sides?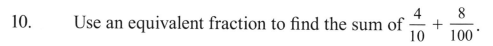

15. $98,406 + 21,597 = ?$

| | | |
|---|---|---|
| **1.** 4.NBT.2 | **2.** 4.NF.3 | **3.** 4.MD.4 |

**3.** 4.MD.4

**Primate Height** (in feet)

|  | 1 | 1½ | 2 | 2½ | 3 | 3½ | 4 |

Lemurs    Long-Nosed Monkey    Chimpanzees

| | | |
|---|---|---|
| **4.** 4.NBT.4 | **5.** 4.NF.4 | **6.** 4.MD.1 |

**6.** 4.MD.1

| lb | oz |
|----|----|
| 1 | 16 |
| 2 |  |
|  | 48 |
| 4 |  |

| | | |
|---|---|---|
| **7.** 4.OA.3 | **8.** 4.NBT.3 | **9.** 4.NF.2 |

**9.** 4.NF.2

$$\frac{8}{14} \bigcirc \frac{11}{14}$$

**10.** 4.NF.5

**11.** 4.NBT.5

A) $(30 \times 50) + (30 \times 7) + (30 \times 50) + (3 \times 7)$

B) $(30 \times 50) + (30 \times 7) + (3 \times 50) + (3 \times 7)$

**12.** 4.MD.3

7 cm

4 cm

**13.** 4.NBT.6

**14.** 4.G.2

**15.** 4.NBT.4

# Lesson #105

1.    $6{,}000 - 4{,}288 = ?$

2.    What is the area of a rectangle with a length of 9 cm and a width of 8 cm?
      Label the answer.

3.    Decompose the mixed number $3\frac{7}{8}$. Rename it in two different ways.

4.    Replace the mixed number with an equivalent fraction. Then, subtract.
      $$1\tfrac{1}{3} - \tfrac{2}{3} \rightarrow 1\tfrac{1}{3} = \tfrac{3}{3} + \tfrac{1}{3} = \tfrac{4}{3}, \text{ so } \tfrac{4}{3} - \tfrac{2}{3} = ?$$

5.    Pencils cost 5¢ each. Alice used nickels to buy her pencils, and she spent $2.10.
      How many nickels did Alice use?

6.    **There are 360° in a circle.** Each section of the circle is
      congruent — the same shape and the same size. Write an
      equation that shows the measure of angle $x$.

      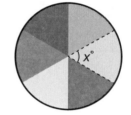

7.    Complete the pattern. 50, 44, 38, 32, _____, _____.
      Describe the pattern.

8.    Round 498,205 to the nearest hundred thousand.

9.    If you placed two of the shortest pencils end-to-end and measured them, what
      would the total length be?

10.   Use a matrix model to find the product: $98 \times 21 = ?$

11.   Which shape has perpendicular sides?   A)⬜   B)◺   C)☆   D)◿

12.   $567{,}819 + 378{,}463 = ?$

13.   Savannah practices her ballet $\dfrac{6}{8}$ of an hour each day. How many hours does she
      practice over 4 days? Is the answer greater or less than four?

14.   $766 \div 6 = ?$

15.   Write the name of the obtuse angle
      in the answer box.

      ∠LID        ∠CAT        ∠DOG        ∠LAP

| | | |
|---|---|---|
| **1.** 4.NBT.4 | **2.** 4.MD.3<br><br>9 cm<br>8 cm | **3.** 4.NF.3 |
| **4.** 4.NF.3 | **5.** 4.MD.2 | **6.** 4.MD.7 |
| **7.** 4.OA.5 | **8.** 4.NBT.3 | **9.** 4.MD.4<br><br>**Pencil Length** (in inches)<br>5½  6  6¼  6½  7  7¼  7½ |
| **10.** 4.NBT.5<br><br>___ + ___ | **11.** 4.G.2 | **12.** 4.NBT.4 |
| **13.** 4.NF.4 | **14.** 4.NBT.6 | **15.** 4.G.1 |

# Lesson #106

1.  Mama Lou uses $\frac{3}{4}$ cup of peppers for each gallon of soup that she makes. How many cups of peppers will she use if she makes 2 gallons of soup? Between what two numbers does your answer lie?

2.  Dr. O'Neil saw 32 patients this week. That was 4 times as many as she saw last week. Choose the best equation and use it to find out how many patients Dr. O'Neil saw last week.

3.  Find the difference. $\frac{5}{5} - \frac{3}{5} = ?$

4.  Fill in the sign that makes this sentence true.

5.  $693,425 + 218,366 = ?$

6.  Which shape has parallel sides?

7.  Find the sum. $\frac{3}{10} + \frac{20}{100} = ?$ Change tenths to hundredths before you add.

8.  Read the table. Fill in the missing values.

9.  What's the difference in length between the longest pencils measured and the shortest?

10. For the equation in the box, which of the following is the best estimate for $x$: 200, 300, or 400?

11. What is the area of the rectangle? Label the answer.

12. Round 575,413 to the nearest hundred thousand.

13. Nolan and Seamus got a new video game. Nolan completed $\frac{4}{12}$ of the game and Seamus completed $\frac{1}{12}$ of the game. How much of the game did the boys complete together?

14. Which shows the use of the distributive property for $45 \times 71$?

15. $16,000 - 8,346 = ?$

| | | |
|---|---|---|
| **1.**      4.NF.4 | **2.**      4.OA.2<br><br>A) $32 \times 4 = p$<br><br>B) $4 \times p = 32$ | **3.**      4.NF.3 |
| **4.**      4.NF.2<br><br><br>$\dfrac{9}{10} \bigcirc \dfrac{9}{12}$ | **5.**      4.NBT.4 | **6.**      4.G.2 |
| **7.**      4.NF.5 | **8.**      4.MD.1 <table><tr><th>L</th><th>mL</th></tr><tr><td>10</td><td>10,000</td></tr><tr><td>20</td><td>20,000</td></tr><tr><td>30</td><td></td></tr><tr><td>40</td><td></td></tr></table> | **9.**      4.MD.4<br><br>**Pencil Length** (in inches)<br><br>x x x   x    x    x   x x x     x x<br>5½   6   6¼   6½   7   7¼   7½ |
| **10.**      4.OA.3<br><br>$76 + 67 + 43 + 124 = x$ | **11.**      4.MD.3<br><br>7 in.<br>⬜ 2 in. | **12.**      4.NBT.3 |
| **13.**      4.NF.3 | **14.**      4.NBT.5<br><br>A) $(40 \times 70) + (40 \times 1) + (5 \times 70) + (5 \times 1)$<br><br>B) $(40 \times 70) + (40 \times 1) + (5 \times 70) + (5 \times 10)$ | **15.**      4.NBT.4 |

# Lesson #107

1.   The fence around the pool was 2.5 meters high. How many centimeters high was the pool fence?

2.   50 girls have been invited to the gymnastics team victory party. They are ordering pizza. How many 8-slice pizzas will they need to have a slice for each girl and how many slices will be left over?

3.   Vince spent $11.25 to purchase 5 bracelets. If all of the bracelets were the same price, how much was each bracelet?

4.   Write the names of the right angles in the answer box.

5.   $832 - 288 = ?$

6.   Decompose the fraction $\frac{7}{10}$. Rename it in two different ways.

7.   Round 23,589 to the nearest ten thousand.

8.   $678,905 + 244,762 = ?$

9.   Write the base-ten number for $40,000 + 5,000 + 600 + 40 + 9$.

10.  Use an equivalent fraction to find the sum. $\frac{2}{10} + \frac{30}{100} = ?$

11.  $810 \div 9 = ?$

12.  Jack practices playing his trumpet $\frac{1}{3}$ hour each day. How many hours will Jack practice over the next 5 days? Between what two numbers does your answer lie?

13.  Complete the pattern. 49, 42, 35, 28, _____, _____. Describe the pattern.

14.  Choose the numbers that are multiples of both 2 and 5.

15.  Find the measure of $\angle XYZ$.

| 1.     4.MD.1 | 2.     4.OA.3 | 3.     4.MD.2 |
|---|---|---|
| 4.     4.G.1 | 5.     4.NBT.4 | 6.     4.NF.3 |
| 7.     4.NBT.3 | 8.     4.NBT.4 | 9.     4.NBT.2 |
| 10.     4.NF.5 | 11.     4.NBT.6 | 12.     4.NF.4 |
| 13.     4.OA.5 | 14.     4.OA.4 <br><br> 10    40    15    20    60 | 15.     4.MD.6 |

# Lesson #108

1. The construction company uses $\frac{7}{8}$ gallon of paint for each wall of the new house they are building. If they paint 8 walls, how many gallons of paint will the construction company use?

2. Neil removed 5 kilograms of clay for his next pottery project. How many grams of clay did Neil remove?

3. $7,321 - 3,498 = ?$

4. Which shows the use of the distributive property for $53 \times 86$?

5. Find the sum. $\frac{1}{10} + \frac{25}{100} = ?$ Change tenths to hundredths before you add.

6. The area of a rectangle is 70 square inches. The length of one of the sides is 10 inches. Find the width. Label the answer. (Remember: $l \times w = Area$)

7. $693,776 + 256,916 = ?$

8. Which shape has perpendicular sides?    A) B) C) D)

9. Choose the sign that makes this sentence true.

10. Find the sum. Remember to rename fractions that have a numerator that is larger than the denominator. Write the sum as a mixed number.

    $\frac{3}{4} + \frac{3}{4} = \frac{6}{4} \rightarrow \frac{6}{4} = \frac{4}{4} + \underline{\quad} = ?$

11. If you stacked the four shortest doors on top of one another, what would the total height be?

12. Morris More is a jeweler. He has a $900 budget for supplies. He already spent $225 on silver and $385 on gold. If gemstones cost about $40 each, what is a good estimate of how many gemstones he can afford with the money left over, 1, 5, or 10?

13. Find the sum. $\frac{4}{12} + \frac{7}{12} = ?$

14. $3,606 \div 5 = ?$

15. Find the measure of $\angle ABC$.

| 1.     4.NF.4 | 2.     4.MD.1 | 3.     4.NBT.4 |
|---|---|---|
| **4.     4.NBT.5**<br><br>A) $(50 \times 80) + (50 \times 6) + (3 \times 8) + (3 \times 6)$<br><br>B) $(50 \times 80) + (50 \times 6) + (3 \times 80) + (3 \times 6)$ | 5.     4.NF.5 | 6.     4.MD.3 |
| 7.     4.NBT.4 | 8.     4.G.2 | 9.     4.NF.2<br><br>$$\frac{8}{10} \bigcirc \frac{6}{10}$$ |
| 10.     4.NF.3 | 11.     4.MD.4<br><br>**Door Height** (in feet)<br><br>3  3½  4  4½  5  5½  6  6½ | 12.     4.OA.3 |
| 13.     4.NF.3 | 14.     4.NBT.6 | 15.     4.MD.6<br> |

# Lesson #109

1. The tractor pulled the wagon 6 kilometers. How many meters did the tractor pull the wagon?

2. Find the measure of $\angle ABC$.

3. $40,000 - 18,271 = ?$

4. Decompose the mixed number $5\frac{3}{4}$. Rename it in two different ways.

5. The area of a rectangle is 10 square centimeters. The length of one of the sides is 5 centimeters. Find the width. Label the answer. (Remember: $l \times w = Area$)

6. Use an equivalent fraction to find the sum of $\frac{9}{10} + \frac{10}{100}$.

7. Round 716,254 to the nearest hundred.

8. What is the difference in height between one of the tallest doors and one of the shortest doors?

9. $397,716 + 562,557 = ?$

10. If six players each drink $\frac{2}{3}$ quart of water during practice, how many quarts of water will the coach need to bring? Draw a fraction model to help you solve the problem.

11. $2,475 \div 7 = ?$

12. A right triangle has exactly one right angle. Circle the right triangle.

13. Lee's grandmother gave him $18.20 to split evenly with his sister. How much money did each child get?

14. Michelle and Claire needed $3\frac{5}{6}$ quarts of paint to make a sign for the football team. Michelle has $1\frac{2}{6}$ quarts and Claire had $2\frac{4}{6}$ quarts of paint. How many quarts of paint do the girls have together? Will it be enough to paint the sign? Explain why or why not.

15. Complete the pattern. 63, 58, 53, 48, _____ , _____. Describe the pattern.

| 1.       4.MD.1 | 2.       4.MD.6 | 3.       4.NBT.4 |
|---|---|---|
| | | |
| 4.       4.NF.3 | 5.       4.MD.3 | 6.       4.NF.5 |
| 7.       4.NBT.3 | 8.       4.MD.4 | 9.       4.NBT.4 |
| | **Door Height** (in feet) | |
| 10.      4.NF.4 | 11.      4.NBT.6 | 12.      4.G.2 |
| | | |
| 13.      4.MD.2 | 14.      4.NF.3 | 15.      4.OA.5 |

# Lesson #110

1. Fill in the sign to make this sentence true.

2. Describe the pattern.

3. A right triangle has exactly one right angle. Circle the right triangle.

4. Jeorge uses $\frac{4}{5}$ foot of tape to wrap his ankle before each football game. If Jeorge has 9 football games this season, how much tape will he need to buy? Draw a fraction model to help you solve the problem.

5. Choose the numbers that are multiples of both 3 and 5.

6. The two rays form a right angle. What is the value of $s$?

7. $8,017 - 2,359 = ?$

8. Find the sum. $\frac{5}{10} + \frac{27}{100} = ?$ Change tenths to hundredths before you add.

9. Find the difference. $\frac{10}{10} - \frac{7}{10} = ?$

10. Round 43,276 to the nearest hundred.

11. $186,612 + 883,214 = ?$

12. What is the difference in height between one of the shortest dogs measured and one of the tallest?

13. Luke spent 5 times as many dollars for a present for his mom than for his brother. He spent 3 dollars on a present for his brother. How much did Luke spend for his mother's present?

14. The area of a rectangle is 18 mm². The width of one of the sides is 6 mm. Find the length. Label the answer. (Remember: $l \times w = Area$)

15. $49 \times 18 = ?$ Complete the matrix model to find the product.

| | | |
|---|---|---|
| **1.**   4.NF.2 <br><br> $$\frac{9}{12} \bigcirc \frac{9}{100}$$ | **2.**   4.OA.5 | **3.**   4.G.2 |
| **4.**   4.NF.4 | **5.**   4.OA.4 <br><br> 15   12   30   18   27 | **6.**   4.MD.7 <br><br> $s°$ $21°$ $43°$ |
| **7.**   4.NBT.4 | **8.**   4.NF.5 | **9.**   4.NF.3 |
| **10.**   4.NBT.3 | **11.**   4.NBT.4 | **12.**   4.MD.4 <br><br> **Dog Height at Shoulder** (in feet) <br><br> ½   1   1⅛   1¼   1½   2   2¼   2½ |
| **13.**   4.OA.1 | **14.**   4.MD.3 | **15.**   4.NBT.5 |

# Lesson #111

1.  Luca rode his bike 40 miles on Monday. That was 4 times as far as he rode on Sunday. How far did Luca ride on Sunday? Choose the correct equation and solve it.

2.  Use an equivalent fraction to find the sum of $\frac{3}{10} + \frac{41}{100}$.

3.  Complete the pattern. 37, 33, 29, 25, _____, _____. Describe the pattern.

4.  Write the sum as a mixed number. $\frac{3}{5} + \frac{4}{5} = \frac{7}{5} \rightarrow \frac{7}{5} = \frac{5}{5} + \frac{\square}{\square} = ?$

5.  Ellie and Easton gave their dog a bath. They filled a bucket with $4\frac{1}{2}$ liters of water. They added 2 liters of water while they were rinsing the dog. How many milliliters of water did they use to wash the dog?

6.  Which shows the use of the distributive property for $39 \times 62$?

7.  $68,704 + 73,325 = ?$

8.  If one of the shortest dogs stood on the other shortest dog's back, what would be the total height of the two dogs?

9.  $4,537 \div 8 = ?$

10. Mrs. Phillips took her daughter and her daughter's friends bowling. There were 7 girls in all. She paid for 25 games. How many games will each girl be able to play and how many games will be left over?

11. The area of a rectangle is 28 m². The length of one of the sides is 4 m. Find the width. Label the answer. (Remember: $l \times w = Area$)

12. Decompose the fraction $\frac{3}{5}$. Rename it in two different ways.

13. Write $50,000 + 6,000 + 400 + 20 + 5$ as a base-ten number.

14. The wedding cake recipe uses 2,500 grams of butter. How many kilograms of butter does the recipe use?

15. Circle the shape that shows both parallel and perpendicular sides. What do we call this shape?

    rectangle          circle          parallelogram          pentagon

| | | |
|---|---|---|
| **1.**    4.OA.2<br><br>A) $40 \div 4 = m$<br><br>B) $40 \times 4 = m$ | **2.**    4.NF.5 | **3.**    4.OA.5 |
| **4.**    4.NF.3<br><br>$\dfrac{5}{5} + \dfrac{\square}{\square} =$ _____ | **5.**    4.MD.2 | **6.**    4.NBT.5<br><br>A) $(30 \times 60) + (30 \times 2) + (9 \times 60) + (9 \times 2)$<br><br>B) $(30 \times 60) + (30 \times 2) + (9 \times 60) + (9 \times 20)$ |
| **7.**    4.NBT.4 | **8.**    4.MD.4<br><br>**Dog Height at Shoulder** (in feet)<br><br>½   1   1⅛   1¼   1½   2   2¼   2½ | **9.**    4.NBT.6 |
| **10.**    4.OA.3 | **11.**    4.MD.3 | **12.**    4.NF.3 |
| **13.**    4.NBT.2 | **14.**    4.MD.1 | **15.**    4.G.2<br><br> |

# Lesson #112

1. Mr. Harold's fifth graders bagged large cans for recycling. They collected 75 cans. Each bag holds 8 cans. How many bags did Mr. Harold's class fill and how many cans were left over?

2. Look at the trapezoid. Which two line segments are parallel? Write their names in the box.

3. Show $\frac{9}{12}$ as the sum of unit fractions.

   ___ + ___ + ___ + ___ + ___ + ___ + ___ + ___ + ___ = ___

4. Fill in the sign to make this sentence true.

5. Describe the pattern.

6. $8,000 - 2,555 = ?$

7. Hollie collects $\frac{5}{8}$ cup of pumpkin seeds from each pumpkin she carves to roast for a snack. This year she carved 3 pumpkins. How many cups of seeds will Hollie have to roast? Draw a fraction model to help you solve the problem.

8. If the height of all the dogs measuring $1\frac{1}{8}$ feet were added together, what would the total height be?

9. Circle the right triangle.

10. Find the measure of $\angle GFE$.

11. $716,248 + 356,303 = ?$

12. The area of a rectangle is 40 cm². The width of one of the sides is 5 cm. Find the length. Label the answer.

13. $\overrightarrow{FE}$ and $\overrightarrow{FG}$ are perpendicular. What is the value of $c$?

14. Which shows the use of the distributive property for $11 \times 71$?

15. Farmer Franny has $15\frac{7}{12}$ yards of soil she needs to till before she can plant her crops. On Monday she tilled $7\frac{2}{12}$ yards and on Tuesday she tilled $4\frac{11}{12}$ yards. How many yards of soil did Franny till over the two days? Did she till enough of the soil to begin planting her crops? Explain why or why not.

| | | |
|---|---|---|
| **1.** 4.OA.3 | **2.** 4.G.1 | **3.** 4.NF.3 |
| **4.** 4.NF.2 $$\frac{5}{11} \bigcirc \frac{4}{11}$$ | **5.** 4.OA.5 | **6.** 4.NBT.4 |
| **7.** 4.NF.4 | **8.** 4.MD.4 **Dog Height at Shoulder** (in feet) ½  1  1⅛  1¼  1½  2  2¼  2½ | **9.** 4.G.2 |
| **10.** 4.MD.6 | **11.** 4.NBT.4 | **12.** 4.MD.3 |
| **13.** 4.MD.7 | **14.** 4.NBT.5  A) $(10 \times 70) + (10 \times 10) + (1 \times 70) + (1 \times 1)$  B) $(10 \times 70) + (10 \times 1) + (1 \times 70) + (1 \times 1)$ | **15.** 4.NF.3 |

# Lesson #113

1.    Write the base-ten number for 40,000 + 7,000 + 300 + 8.

2.    Carmen planted a sunflower for his grandmother. The flower grew $\frac{4}{12}$ of an inch each day for 5 days in a row. How tall was the sunflower after the 5th day? Draw a fraction model to help you solve the problem.

3.    The book was so good that Charlene read the whole thing in 2 hours. How many minutes did it take Charlene to read the book?

4.    Barry fed the elephants 3 times as many bags of peanuts as he fed the monkeys. He fed the monkeys 7 bags of peanuts. How many bags of peanuts did Barry feed the elephants?

5.    Find the measure of $\angle CBA$.

6.    358,255 + 733,498 = ?

7.    Find the sum. $\frac{4}{10} + \frac{31}{100} = ?$ Change tenths to hundredths before you add.

8.    Cold Comfort sells four flavors of ice cream. On Monday, they sell 148 vanilla cones, 125 chocolate cones, 62 peach cones, and 175 strawberry cones. If they sell the same this week, how many cones will the company have sold in all?

9.    Greg went into the hobby store with $14.50. He came out with $2.23. How much money did he spend at the hobby store?

10.   $3,078 \div 5 = ?$

11.   Sam is in first grade and gets 10 minutes of homework a night. His brother, Jeffery, is in fourth grade. He gets three times more homework than Sam. How many minutes of homework does Jeffery get each night? Write a number sentence and solve it.

12.   403 − 179 = ?

13.   Decompose the mixed number $4\frac{6}{12}$. Rename it in two different ways.

14.   Circle the shape that has perpendicular sides that form exactly two right angles.

15.   Choose the numbers that are multiples of both 3 and 4.

| | | |
|---|---|---|
| **1.**     4.NBT.2 | **2.**     4.NF.4 | **3.**     4.MD.1 |
| **4.**     4.OA.1 | **5.**     4.MD.6 | **6.**     4.NBT.4 |
| **7.**     4.NF.5 | **8.**     4.OA.3 | **9.**     4.MD.2 |
| **10.**     4.NBT.6 | **11.**     4.OA.2 | **12.**     4.NBT.4 |
| **13.**     4.NF.3 | **14.**     4.G.2 | **15.**     4.OA.4     15    16    48    33    12 |

# Lesson #114

1.  Find the sum. $\dfrac{7}{10} + \dfrac{15}{100} = ?$ Change tenths to hundredths before you add.

2.  Circle the right triangle.

3.  If $\angle MNP$ is a straight angle, what is the value of $a + b$?

4.  The area of a rectangle is 54 mm². The length of one of the sides is 9 mm. Find the width. Label the answer.

5.  The faucet leaked 5,500 milliliters of water before it was turned off. How many liters of water leaked from the faucet?

6.  If you stacked the tallest and shortest items end-to-end and measured them, what would the total length be?

7.  Use the distributive property to multiply $59 \times 41$.

8.  Find the sum. $\dfrac{27}{100} + \dfrac{12}{100} = ?$

9.  $3,456 \div 6 = ?$

10. $129,465 + 452,727 = ?$

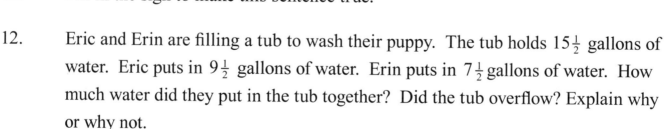

11. Fill in the sign to make this sentence true.

12. Eric and Erin are filling a tub to wash their puppy. The tub holds $15\frac{1}{2}$ gallons of water. Eric puts in $9\frac{1}{2}$ gallons of water. Erin puts in $7\frac{1}{2}$ gallons of water. How much water did they put in the tub together? Did the tub overflow? Explain why or why not.

13. Judy makes bracelets by stringing beads. She has 66 silver beads and each bracelet needs 8 silver beads. How many bracelets can she make and how many silver beads will be left over?

14. Complete the pattern. 5, 13, 21, 29, ____, ____. Describe the pattern.

15. Round 813,491 to the nearest hundred thousand.

| 1.          4.NF.5 | 2.          4.G.2 | 3.          4.MD.7 |
|---|---|---|

| 4.          4.MD.3 | 5.          4.MD.1 | 6.          4.MD.4 |
|---|---|---|

**Length of School Supplies** (in inches)

¼  ½  1  1⅛  1¼  1½  2  2⅛  2¼

| 7.          4.NBT.5 | 8.          4.NF.3 | 9.          4.NBT.6 |
|---|---|---|

| 10.          4.NBT.4 | 11.          4.NF.2 | 12.          4.NF.3 |
|---|---|---|

$$\frac{2}{10} \bigcirc \frac{2}{8}$$

| 13.          4.OA.3 | 14.          4.OA.5 | 15.          4.NBT.3 |
|---|---|---|

# Lesson #115

1.  Round 34,615 to the nearest ten thousand.

2.  $86,214 + 34,556 = ?$

3.  Circle the shape that has exactly two sets of parallel sides.  Name this shape.

4.  Use the distributive property to multiply $35 \times 72$.

5.  $70,000 - 56,243 = ?$

6.  The popcorn finished popping in the microwave in 270 seconds.  How many minutes did it take the popcorn to pop?

7.  What is the difference in length between the longest item and the 1″ item?

8.  Find the sum.  Remember to rename fractions that have a numerator that is larger than the denominator.  Write the sum as a mixed number.

    $$\frac{3}{8} + \frac{7}{8} = \frac{10}{8} \rightarrow \frac{10}{8} = \frac{8}{8} + \frac{\square}{\square} = ?$$

9.  In the box, write the name of each object next to its description.

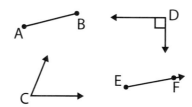

10.  8,165 divided by 5 = ?

11.  Postal Carrier Pete delivered 108 packages this afternoon.  That is 9 times as many as he delivered this morning.  Choose the best equation and use it to find out how many packages he delivered this morning.

12.  Enya D. Weems sells dream potions.  The last four days, she's made $127, $198, $283, and $202.  She needs to make $900 to pay her rent.  About how much more must she make, $100, $200, or $300?

13.  Jessica feeds her pet fish $\frac{1}{2}$ teaspoon of fish flakes each day.  How many teaspoons will Jessica feed her fish over 8 days?  Draw a fraction model to help you solve the problem.

14.  Use an equivalent fraction to find the sum of $\frac{8}{10} + \frac{26}{100}$.

15.  Find the measure of $\angle QPO$.

| 1. 4.NBT.3 | 2. 4.NBT.4 | 3. 4.G.2 |
|---|---|---|
| | | |

| 4. 4.NBT.5 | 5. 4.NBT.4 | 6. 4.MD.1 |
|---|---|---|
| | | |

| 7. 4.MD.4 | 8. 4.NF.3 | 9. 4.G.1 |
|---|---|---|
| **Length of School Supplies** (in inches) | $\dfrac{8}{8} + \dfrac{\square}{\square} = $ ____ | Acute Angle _____<br>Line Segment _____<br>Ray _____<br>Right Angle _____ |

| 10. 4.NBT.6 | 11. 4.OA.2 | 12. 4.OA.3 |
|---|---|---|
| | A) $108 \times 9 = p$<br><br>B) $9 \times p = 108$ | |

| 13. 4.NF.4 | 14. 4.NF.5 | 15. 4.MD.6 |
|---|---|---|
| | | |

# Lesson #116

1. Eunice went to the concession stand to buy a ring pop for 60¢. She only had nickels. How many did she use?

2. The fraction $\frac{53}{100}$ can be rewritten as the decimal 0.53. Write $\frac{87}{100}$ as a decimal.

3. Find the sum. $\frac{3}{10} + \frac{64}{100} = ?$  Change tenths to hundredths before you add.

4. Write the name of the acute angle in the box.

   ∠DEA        ∠FBI        ∠NSA        ∠CIA

5. Round 86,342 to the nearest hundred.

6. Find the difference. $\frac{2}{2} - \frac{1}{2} = ?$

7. Describe the pattern.

8. Write the base-ten number for 40,000 + 5,000 + 60 + 4.

9. Decompose the fraction $\frac{10}{12}$. Rename it in two different ways.

10. 868,771 + 236,439 = ?

11. What is the difference in length between the longest road measured in Jefferson County and the shortest road measured in Petrie County?

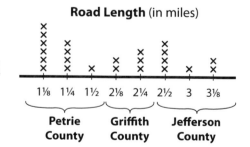

12. 605 − 176 = ?

13. Blake dove 3 feet underwater. How many inches did Blake dive?

14. Fill in the sign to make this sentence true.

15. Use a matrix model to find the product:  54 × 47 = ?

| 1.     4.MD.2 | 2.     4.NF.6 | 3.     4.NF.5 |
|---|---|---|
| 4.     4.G.1 | 5.     4.NBT.3 | 6.     4.NF.3 |
| 7.     4.OA.5 | 8.     4.NBT.2 | 9.     4.NF.3 |
| 10.     4.NBT.4 | 11.     4.MD.4 | 12.     4.NBT.4 |
| 13.     4.MD.1 | 14.     4.NF.2 $\dfrac{5}{16} \bigcirc \dfrac{7}{16}$ | 15.     4.NBT.5 |

# Lesson #117

1.  Jaynelle walked 12 feet to her bus stop. How many yards did Jaynelle walk?

2.  The seed envelope said that the sunflower would grow $14\frac{2}{10}$ inches high. The first week the sunflower grew $4\frac{9}{10}$ inches. The second week the sunflower grew $6\frac{4}{10}$. How many inches did the sunflower grow over the two weeks? Is the sunflower as tall as the seed envelope said it would be yet? Explain why or why not.

3.  Circle the right triangle.

4.  Each section of the circle is congruent with all the others. Write an equation that shows the measure of angle $y$.

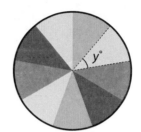

5.  4,738 divided by 6 = ?

6.  Use an equivalent fraction to find the sum of $\frac{4}{10}+\frac{28}{100}$.

7.  Carter is a little league pitcher. He equally practices 5 types of pitches. If he pitches the ball 47 times, how many times will he practice each pitch?

8.  The area of a rectangle is 56 in.². The length of one of the sides is 7 in. Find the width. Label the answer.

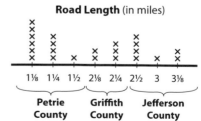

9.  34,554 + 76,386 = ?

10. 41,216 − 3,755 = ?

11. Write $\frac{97}{100}$ as a decimal.

12. Aiden rides the bus $\frac{4}{5}$ of a mile each day to school. For how many miles will Aiden be on the bus after 5 days? Draw a fraction model to help you solve the problem.

13. If all of the roads in Griffith County were laid end to end, what would the total length be?

14. Round 367,851 to the nearest hundred thousand.

15. Señora Romina filled 7 vases with water. Each vase held 1 liter of water. In milliliters, how much water did Señora Romina use to fill the vases?

| | | |
|---|---|---|
| **1.** 4.MD.1 | **2.** 4.NF.3 | **3.** 4.G.2 |
| **4.** 4.MD.7 | **5.** 4.NBT.6 | **6.** 4.NF.5 |
| **7.** 4.OA.3 | **8.** 4.MD.3 | **9.** 4.NBT.4 |
| **10.** 4.NBT.4 | **11.** 4.NF.6 | **12.** 4.NF.4 |
| **13.** 4.MD.4 | **14.** 4.NBT.3 | **15.** 4.MD.2 |

# Lesson #118

1.    In one week, Joy did homework for twice as many hours as she watched television. She watched television for 7 hours. How many hours did she do homework?

2.    Write the sum as a mixed number. $\frac{4}{10}+\frac{8}{10}=\frac{12}{10} \rightarrow \frac{12}{10}=\frac{10}{10}+\frac{\Box}{\Box}=?$

3.    Fill in the sign to make the sentence true.

4.    Each angle of the trapezoid to the right is marked with a letter. In your box, write each letter on the correct line to show the type of angle.

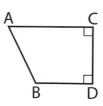

5.    Write the numbers that are multiples of both 3 and 5.

6.    What is the difference in length between the shortest road in Griffith County and the shortest road in Petrie County?

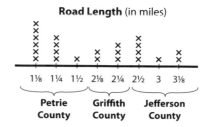

7.    $8,075 - 3,275 = ?$

8.    Sen Shunt is a hard working robot. He performs 30 tasks every weekday and 170 tasks a day on the weekend. How many tasks does he complete in two weeks?

9.    After the snowstorm the snow measured 3 yards deep in the drifts. How many inches deep was the snow?

10.    $4,325 + 8,776 = ?$

11.    Use the distributive property to multiply $86 \times 32$.

12.    Write $\frac{5}{10}$ as a decimal.

13.    Round 462,782 to the nearest hundred thousand.

14.    Tessa's mom spent $96 at the grocery store. That was 2 times as much as she spent last week. How much money did Tessa's mom spend at the grocery store last week? Write an equation with $n$ as the unknown and solve it.

15.    Find the sum. $\frac{5}{10}+\frac{34}{100}=?$ Change tenths to hundredths before you add.

| 1.      4.OA.1 | 2.      4.NF.3 | 3.      4.NF.2 |
|---|---|---|
| | $\dfrac{10}{10} + \dfrac{\Box}{\Box} = $ \_\_\_\_ | $\dfrac{4}{10} \bigcirc \dfrac{4}{100}$ |
| 4.      4.G.1 <br><br> Acute    _____ <br><br> Obtuse    _____ <br><br> Right    _____ | 5.      4.OA.4 <br><br> 25    60    33    10    15 | 6.      4.MD.4 |
| 7.      4.NBT.4 | 8.      4.OA.3 | 9.      4.MD.2 |
| 10.      4.NBT.4 | 11.      4.NBT.5 | 12.      4.NF.6 |
| 13.      4.NBT.3 | 14.      4.OA.2 | 15.      4.NF.5 |

# Lesson #119

1.    Tabitha needs 600 stickers. She collected 224 in May, 110 in June, and 186 in July. She wants to know how many more she must collect. Let $x$ be the unknown number. Which equation below represents the problem?

2.    Write $\frac{23}{100}$ as a decimal.

3.    Write 45,317 in expanded form.

4.    $\overrightarrow{UT}$ and $\overrightarrow{UV}$ are perpendicular. What is the value of $b$?

5.    Show $\frac{3}{4}$ as the sum of unit fractions. _____ + _____ + _____ = _____

6.    The area of a rectangle is 32 cm². The width of one of the sides is 4 cm. Find the length. Label the answer.

7.    $386 + 798 = ?$

8.    $4,525 \div 7 = ?$

9.    $90,000 - 49,773 = ?$

10.   Maté needed school supplies. He spent 50¢ on filler paper, $1.25 on pencils, $4.60 on crayons, and $3.00 on notebooks. How much money did Maté spend on school supplies?

11.   Use an equivalent fraction to find the sum of $\frac{1}{10} + \frac{90}{100}$.

12.   Circle the shape that has both parallel and perpendicular sides. Name this shape.

13.   Use the distributive property to multiply $62 \times 30$.

14.   Leo and Josie had a roll of plastic table cloth that was $15\frac{6}{8}$ feet long. Leo covered a table that was $6\frac{2}{8}$ feet and Josie covered a table that was $6\frac{1}{8}$ feet long. How much plastic table cloth did Leo and Josie use together? Did they have enough plastic table cloth? Explain why or why not.

15.   Write $\frac{5}{12} + \frac{5}{12} + \frac{5}{12} + \frac{5}{12} + \frac{5}{12}$ as a multiplication problem. Then, find the product.

| 1. 4.OA.3 | 2. 4.NF.6 | 3. 4.NBT.2 |
|---|---|---|
| A) $x = 600 - 224 - 110 - 186$  <br><br> B) $x - 600 = 224 + 110 + 186$ | | |

| 4. 4.MD.7 | 5. 4.NF.3 | 6. 4.MD.3 |
|---|---|---|
| | | |

| 7. 4.NBT.4 | 8. 4.NBT.6 | 9. 4.NBT.4 |
|---|---|---|
| | | |

| 10. 4.MD.2 | 11. 4.NF.5 | 12. 4.G.2 |
|---|---|---|
| | | |

| 13. 4.NBT.5 | 14. 4.NF.3 | 15. 4.NF.4 |
|---|---|---|
| | | |

# Lesson #120

1. Grammy Josephina made chicken soup for the family. She used 1 liter of water and 850 milliliters of chicken broth. How many milliliters of liquid did Grammy put in the pot of soup?

2. Read the table. Fill in the missing values.

3. Find the measure of $\angle SRQ$.

4. Circle the right triangle.

5. What is the difference in length between the longest Type B fish and the shortest Type A fish?

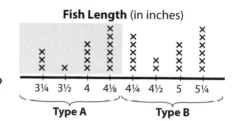

**Fish Length** (in inches)

Type A    Type B

6. $455 \div 5 = ?$

7. Fill in the sign to make this sentence true.

8. Decompose the mixed number $4\frac{4}{6}$. Rename it in two different ways.

9. Complete the pattern. 36, 45, 54, 63, _____, _____. Describe the pattern.

10. Write $\frac{7}{10}$ as a decimal.

11. Fill in the sign that makes this number sentence true.    44,455 ◯ 45,455
    The numbers are the same until the _____ place.

12. Find the sum. $\frac{6}{10} + \frac{21}{100} = ?$ Change tenths to hundredths before you add.

13. $635,215 + 462,771 = ?$

14. $6,123 - 3,765 = ?$

15. Laura walks her dog $\frac{2}{5}$ of a mile three days a week. How many miles does Laura walk each week? Draw a fraction model to help you solve the problem.

| 1.     4.MD.2 | 2.     4.MD.1 | 3.     4.MD.6 |
|---|---|---|
|  | | m | cm |<br>|---|---|<br>| 2.5 | 250 |<br>| 3 | |<br>| 3.5 | | |  |

| m | cm |
|---|---|
| 2.5 | 250 |
| 3 | |
| 3.5 | |

**4.**     4.G.2          **5.**     4.MD.4          **6.**     4.NBT.6

**7.**     4.NF.2          **8.**     4.NF.3          **9.**     4.OA.5

$$\frac{3}{8} \bigcirc \frac{2}{8}$$

**10.**     4.NF.6          **11.**     4.NBT.2          **12.**     4.NF.5

A) ones

B) tens

C) hundreds

D) thousands

**13.**     4.NBT.4          **14.**     4.NBT.4          **15.**     4.NF.4

# Lesson #121

1.    Describe the pattern.

2.    Replace the mixed number with an equivalent fraction.  Then, subtract.

$$1\frac{6}{12} - \frac{9}{12} \rightarrow 1\frac{6}{12} = \frac{12}{12} + \frac{6}{12} = \frac{18}{12} \quad so, \quad \frac{18}{12} - \frac{9}{12} = ?$$

3.    Draw a model to show that $0.4 > 0.1$.  Sketch two models that are about the same size.  Each model is divided into 10 equal shares.  Shade each to show that four-tenths is greater than one-tenth.

4.    The package weighed 6,500 grams.  How many kilograms did the package weigh?

5.    Use an equivalent fraction to find the sum of $\frac{9}{10} + \frac{1}{100}$.

6.    $612 - 498 = ?$

7.    Find the measure of $\angle FED$.

8.    $427 \div 6 = ?$

9.    The area of a rectangular sandbox is 18 m².  The border around the sandbox is 18 m.  What is the length and width of the sandbox?  Use the factor pairs of 18 to help you find the length and width of the sandbox.

10.    Which letter represents 0.76 on the number line?

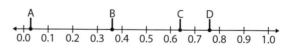

11.    Use a matrix model to find the product:   $45 \times 58 = ?$

12.    Write the numbers that are multiples of both 2 and 9.

13.    Allen A. Dayswork is a busy store manager.  He tracks sales of soda for four days.  The amounts are $187, $245, $123, and $165.  Were soda sales above or below $800?

14.    Dr. Kennedy recorded the lengths of various insects.  Help Dr. Kennedy to organize her data into a line plot.

15.    If Dr. Kennedy placed the three shortest bugs end-to-end and measured them, what would the total length be?

| Insect | Length (in.) |
|---|---|
| Ant 1 | ½ |
| Cricket | 1 |
| Jewel Beetle | 1⅛ |
| Drone Bee | ¼ |
| Ant 2 | ¼ |
| Assassin Bug | 1⅛ |
| Queen Bee | 1 |
| Drone Bee 2 | ½ |

**1.** 4.OA.5

**2.** 4.NF.3

**3.** 4.NF.7

**4.** 4.MD.1

**5.** 4.NF.5

**6.** 4.NBT.4

**7.** 4.MD.6

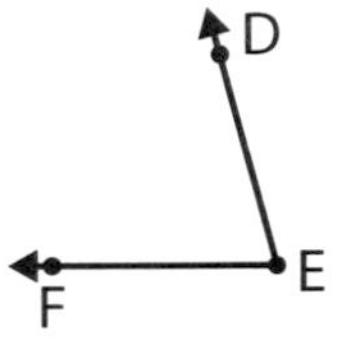


**8.** 4.NBT.6

**9.** 4.MD.3

**10.** 4.NF.6

**11.** 4.NBT.5

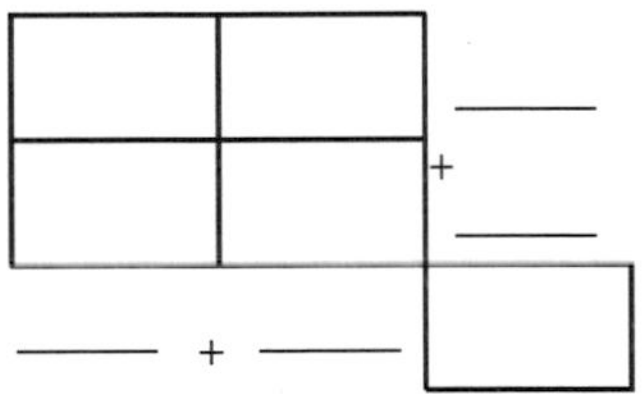


**12.** 4.OA.4

63　18　16　72　2

**13.** 4.OA.3

**14 – 15.** 4.MD.4

# Lesson #122

1. A professional baseball bat weighs about 2 pounds. A tee ball bat weighs about 14 ounces. In ounces, how much more does the professional bat weigh?

2. Write 35,217 in expanded form.

3. Fill in the sign to make this sentence true.

4. The area of a rectangular pool is 12 m². The border around the pool is 16 m. What is the length and width of the pool? Use the factor pairs of 12 to help you find the length and width of the pool.

5. Find the sum. $\frac{1}{10} + \frac{87}{100} = ?$    Change tenths to hundredths before you add.

6. Mama Santo puts $\frac{3}{6}$ cup of green peppers on every pizza she makes. Today she made 4 pizzas. How many cups of peppers did Mama Santo use? Draw a fraction model to help you solve the problem.

7. Draw a model to show that 0.3 < 0.5

8. Study the table. The bakery's bread recipe calls for two and a half pounds of flour. How many ounces is that?

9. 372,446 + 753,279 = ?

10. 6,000 − 2,553 = ?

11. Which letter represents 0.68 on the number line?

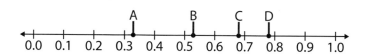

12. Jeff started a dog walking service. He has 49 minutes to walk dogs after school and each dog takes 9 minutes to walk. Walking one dog at a time, how many dogs can Jeff walk in that time and how many minutes would be left over?

13. Complete the pattern. 24, 36, 48, 60, ____ , ____. Describe the pattern.

14. Anita recorded the heights of the many clown figurines in her grandmother's home. Help Anita to organize her data into a line plot.

15. The shortest two clown figurines are designed to stack one on top of the other. When stacked, are they taller or shorter than the tallest figurine? By how much?

| Figurine | Height (in.) |
|---|---|
| Mopey Clown | 3 |
| Hero Clown | 3½ |
| Blue Clown | 4½ |
| Music Clown | 4 |
| Clown Baby | 1½ |
| Broom Clown | 3 |
| Heart Clown | 3½ |
| Clown Father | 2½ |

| 1.  4.MD.2 | 2.  4.NBT.2 | 3.  4.NF.2 |
|---|---|---|
| | | $\dfrac{7}{12} \bigcirc \dfrac{7}{8}$ |

| 4.  4.MD.3 | 5.  4.NF.5 | 6.  4.NF.4 |
|---|---|---|
| | | |

| 7.  4.NF.7 | 8.  4.MD.1 | 9.  4.NBT.4 |
|---|---|---|

**8.**

| lb | oz |
|---|---|
| 1 | 16 |
| 1.5 | 24 |
| 2 | 32 |
| 2.5 | 40 |
| 3 | 48 |

| 10.  4.NBT.4 | 11.  4.NF.6 | 12.  4.OA.3 |
|---|---|---|
| | | |

**13.  4.OA.5**

**14 – 15.  4.MD.4**

0 ———————————————— 4½

# Lesson #123

1.  Consuela has $5\frac{1}{6}$ pies left over from her club's bake sale. She keeps $1\frac{4}{6}$ pies for her family and donates the rest to her local food kitchen. How many pies does the food kitchen receive? Use the visual model to help you.

    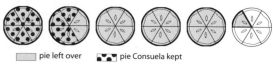

    □ pie left over      ▨ pie Consuela kept

2.  Complete the pattern. 41, 36, 31, ____, ____, ____.
    Describe the pattern.

3.  Use an equivalent fraction to find the sum of $\dfrac{4}{10}+\dfrac{7}{100}$.

4.  Study the table. Fill in the missing values.

5.  Oscar Goldman watched 210 minutes of movie awards shows in January and 290 minutes in February. If he watches the combined amount of those two months in December, how many hours will he have watched in total?

6.  $298,476 + 582,535 = ?$

7.  Draw a model to show that $0.6 > 0.2$.

8.  Find the measure of $\angle PON$.

9.  $7,622 - 3,819 = ?$

10. Which letter represents 0.34 on the number line?

    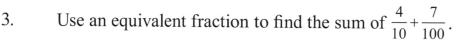

11. Use a matrix model to find the product: $36 \times 69 = ?$

12. If $\angle CDE$ is a straight angle and $\angle CDB$ and $\angle BDE$ are right angles, what is the value of $x$? What is the value of $x + y$?

13. Circle the shape that has perpendicular sides. Name this shape.

    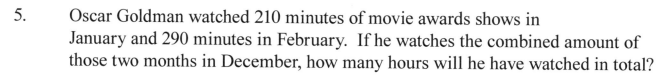

14. Thomas recorded the lengths of several branches he found outside. Help Thomas to organize his data into a line plot.

15. What is the difference in length between the longest branch and the shortest?

| Branch | Length (in.) |
| --- | --- |
| White Oak | 4¼ |
| Black Maple | 5½ |
| Sycamore | 4¼ |
| Buckeye | 4 |
| Douglas Fir | 5½ |
| Ash | 5 |
| River Birch | 4¼ |
| Linden | 5½ |

| 1.  4.NF.3 | 2.  4.OA.5 | 3.  4.NF.5 |
|---|---|---|
| 4.  4.MD.1 | 5.  4.OA.3 | 6.  4.NBT.4 |
| 7.  4.NF.7 | 8.  4.MD.6 | 9.  4.NBT.4 |
| 10.  4.NF.6 | 11.  4.NBT.5 | 12.  4.MD.7 |
| 13.  4.G.2 | 14 – 15.  4.MD.4 | |

**4.** 4.MD.1

| hr | min |
|---|---|
| 1 | 60 |
| 2 | |
| 3 | |

**8.** 4.MD.6

P, O, N

**12.** 4.MD.7

B, C, D, E, $x°$, $y°$, 35°

**14 – 15.** 4.MD.4

4 ———————————— 6

# Lesson #124

1. The area of a rectangular shirt box is 40 square inches. The border around the shirt box is 26 in. What is the length and width of the shirt box? Use the factor pairs of 40 to help you find the length and width of the shirt box.

2. Which letter represents 0.65 on the number line?

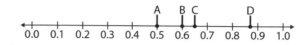

3. Iryna recycles $\frac{3}{4}$ of each magazine she reads. She read 4 magazines this week. How many magazines did Iryna recycle this week? Draw a fraction model to help you solve the problem.

4. Find the sum. Remember to rename fractions that have a numerator that is larger than the denominator. Write the sum as a mixed number.

$$\frac{2}{3}+\frac{2}{3}=\frac{4}{3} \rightarrow \frac{4}{3}=\frac{3}{3}+\frac{\square}{\square}=?$$

5. The candy store sells 6 gumballs in a tube. They have 50 gumballs. How many tubes can they fill and how many gumballs will be left over?

6. Find the sum. $\frac{3}{10}+\frac{67}{100}=?$ Change tenths to hundredths before you add.

7. $3,416 \div 8 = ?$

8. Find the measure of $\angle EDC$.

9. $3,751 + 7,866 = ?$

10. $4,201 - 2,759 = ?$

11. Use the distributive property to multiply $42 \times 76$.

12. Fill in the sign to make this sentence true.

13. Draw a model to show that $0.9 > 0.8$.

14. Terrence recorded the heights of several flowers in his father's greenhouse. Help Terrence to organize his data into a line plot.

| Flower | Height (in.) |
| --- | --- |
| Anemone | 9¼ |
| Rain Lily | 8 |
| Bluebell | 8¼ |
| Fritillaria | 8½ |
| Hyacinth | 9½ |
| Colchium | 9½ |
| Daffodil | 8¼ |
| Allium | 8½ |

15. If Terrence were to cut the longest and the shortest flowers and lay them end-to-end, what would the total length be?

| | | |
|---|---|---|
| **1.** 4.MD.3 | **2.** 4.NF.6 | **3.** 4.NF.4 |
| **4.** 4.NF.3 $\dfrac{3}{3} + \dfrac{\square}{\square} = $ _____ | **5.** 4.OA.3 | **6.** 4.NF.5 |
| **7.** 4.NBT.6 | **8.** 4.MD.6 | **9.** 4.NBT.4 |
| **10.** 4.NBT.4 | **11.** 4.NBT.5 | **12.** 4.NF.2 $\dfrac{10}{22} \bigcirc \dfrac{12}{22}$ |
| **13.** 4.NF.7 | **14 – 15.** 4.MD.4 | |

# Lesson #125

1. Fill in the sign that makes the sentence true. 0.6 ◯ 0.60

2. The fabric store has $9\frac{1}{2}$ yards of muslin on a bolt. Bianca buys $2\frac{1}{2}$ yards. After Martin buys x number of yards, the bolt has $1\frac{1}{2}$ yards remaining. How many yards of muslin did Martin buy? Use the visual model to help you.

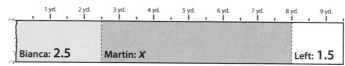

3. Yadier's Little League bag weighs 1 pound empty. If he packs a bat that weighs 20 ounces, a baseball that weighs 5 ounces, and a baseball glove that weighs 14 ounces, how many ounces will the bag weigh?

4. Write $\frac{32}{100}$ as a decimal.

5. $3,165 \div 4 = ?$

6. $3,523 - 1,462 = ?$

7. Read the table. Fill in the missing values.

8. Peggy Hall has a goal of saving $1,000 in five months by using coupons. In the past four months, she's saved $245, $168, $332, and $205. Can she reach her goal by saving less than $100?

9. Complete the pattern. 15, 22, 29, 36, ____, ____. Describe the pattern.

10. Use an equivalent fraction to find the sum of $\frac{2}{10} + \frac{54}{100} = ?$

11. Decompose the fraction $\frac{11}{12}$. Rename it in two different ways.

12. Round 18,563 to the nearest thousand.

13. Noah used $\frac{2}{6}$ can of spray paint to paint a chair. He painted 6 chairs. How many cans of paint did Noah use for painting the chairs? Draw a fraction model to help you solve the problem.

14. Help Michael to organize his garden data into a line plot.

15. What is the difference in length between the longest of the vegetables and the shortest?

| Item | Length (in.) |
| --- | --- |
| Red Pepper | 5¼ |
| Green Pepper | 5½ |
| Potato | 5¼ |
| Asparagus | 6½ |
| Pole Bean | 6¼ |
| Eggplant | 7½ |

| 1.    4.NF.7 | 2.    4.NF.3 | 3.    4.MD.2 |
|---|---|---|
| 4.    4.NF.6 | 5.    4.NBT.6 | 6.    4.NBT.4 |

**7.    4.MD.1**

| min | sec |
|---|---|
|  | 60 |
| 1.5 | 90 |
| 2 |  |

**8.    4.OA.3**

**9.    4.OA.5**

| 10.    4.NF.5 | 11.    4.NF.3 | 12.    4.NBT.3 |
|---|---|---|

**13.    4.NF.4**

**14 – 15.    4.MD.4**

# Lesson #126

1.   Annie Hill took 115 photographs in May, 150 in June, and 150 in July. In August, she takes as many as she took in June and July combined. If 100 pictures were out of focus, how many were in focus?

2.   Fill in the sign to make this sentence true.

3.   Round 834,275 to the nearest hundred.

4.   $4,317 \div 6 = ?$

5.   Use the distributive property to multiply $37 \times 87$.

6.   Find the sum.  $\frac{3}{5} + \frac{1}{5} = ?$

7.   $80,000 - 28,444 = ?$

8.   Circle the shape that has parallel sides. Name this shape.

9.   Complete the pattern.  31, 29, 27, 25, ____, ____. Describe the pattern.

10.  Which letter represents 0.51 on the number line?

11.  Read the table. Fill in the missing values.

12.  Fill in the sign that makes the sentence true.    0.05 ◯ 0.5

13.  $347,885 + 793,264 = ?$

14.  Coco is throwing a soup social. She makes $1\frac{3}{10}$ liters of soup. Her visitors bring a total of $5\frac{5}{10}$ liters of soup. Altogether, $4\frac{4}{10}$ liters of soup are eaten. How much is left over? Part of a visual model is provided for you. Complete the visual model to help you.

15.  Find the sum.  $\frac{5}{10} + \frac{14}{100} = ?$ Change tenths to hundredths before you add.

**1.** 4.OA.3

**2.** 4.NF.2

$$\frac{6}{10} \bigcirc \frac{6}{6}$$

**3.** 4.NBT.3

**4.** 4.NBT.6

**5.** 4.NBT.5

**6.** 4.NF.3

**7.** 4.NBT.4

**8.** 4.G.2

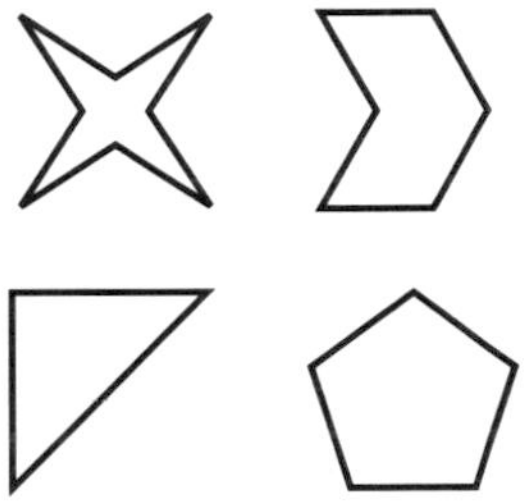

**9.** 4.OA.5

**10.** 4.NF.6

**11.** 4.MD.1

| feet | inches |
|---|---|
| 4.5 | |
| 5 | 60 |
| | 66 |

**12.** 4.NF.7

**13.** 4.NBT.4

**14.** 4.NF.3

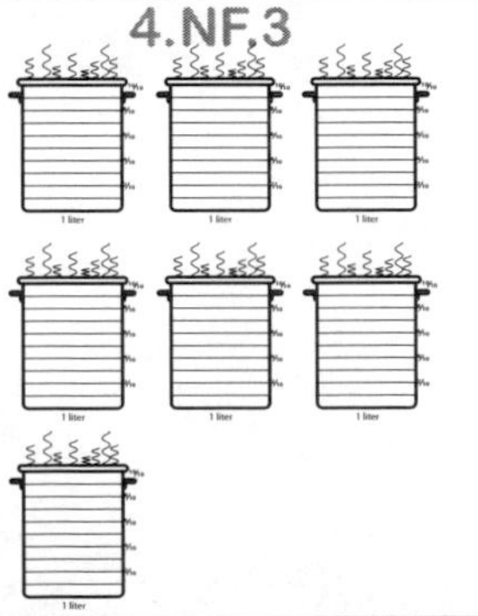

**15.** 4.NF.5

# Lesson #127

1.  Find the area of the shape. The dotted line helps to show two different rectangles. Find the area of each rectangle, and then add them together for a total.

2.  Farmer Mario is getting older and wants to sell some of his farm land. Of his original $10\frac{1}{3}$ acres, he sells $2\frac{1}{3}$ acres to Farmer Ay and $x$ acres to Farmer Bee. Farmer Mario is left with $3\frac{2}{3}$ acres. How many acres did Farmer Bee buy? Use the visual model to help you.

3.  Fill in the sign that makes the sentence true.    0.23 $\bigcirc$ 0.74

4.  Paul built a model train set for his basement. He used $\frac{1}{3}$ tube of glue for each of the train cars he built. The model train had 7 cars. How many tubes of glue did Paul use? Draw a fraction model to help you solve the problem.

5.  Read the table to the right. Fill in the missing values.

6.  Replace the mixed number with an equivalent fraction. Then, subtract.

    $$1\frac{1}{6} - \frac{5}{6} \rightarrow 1\frac{1}{6} = \frac{6}{6} + \frac{1}{6} = \frac{7}{6} \text{ so, } \frac{7}{6} - \frac{5}{6} = ?$$

7.  Elaine made smoothies for her family. She added fruit to 1 liter of milk and 250 milliliters of apple juice. How many milliliters of milk and juice did Elaine use to make the smoothies?

8.  Write $\frac{12}{100}$ as a decimal.

9.  $259 \div 9 = ?$

10. Round 8,574 to the nearest thousand.

11. $824 - 638 = ?$

12. $74,336 + 81,525 = ?$

13. Circle the right triangle.

14. Use an equivalent fraction to find the sum of $\frac{6}{10} + \frac{9}{100}$.

15. Write the numbers that are multiples of both 3 and 5.

| 1. 4.MD.3 | 2. 4.NF.3 | 3. 4.NF.7 |
|---|---|---|

**1.** 4.MD.3

10 in.

3 in.           2 in.

5 in.

**5.** 4.MD.1

| yards | feet |
|---|---|
| 1 | 3 |
|  | 6 |
| 3 |  |

**15.** 4.OA.4

45    15    20    60    21

# Lesson #128

1. Write 34,215 in expanded form.

2. This summer, Brandon and his 2 brothers cut Mrs. Thompson's grass. At the end of the season, she gave the boys $27.33 to split evenly. How much money did each boy get?

3. $347,816 + 417,396 = ?$

4. The decimal 0.82 represents _____ tenths and _____ hundredths.

5. Each box of fudge has 7 equally-sized slices in it. Greg takes $2\frac{3}{7}$ boxes worth of fudge, Antoine takes $3\frac{5}{7}$, and Gilda takes the rest. If there were originally 8 boxes, how many boxes worth of fudge does Gilda get? Use the visual model to help you.

6. Use a protractor to draw a 160° angle. Label it $\angle YUI$.

7. Fill in the sign to make this sentence true.

8. $400 - 253 = ?$

9. $721 \div 6 = ?$

10. Bob likes to jump rope. The first day he jumped 9 times in a row. The second day he made 6 more jumps in a row than he did the first. How many times did he jump the second day?

11. Wanda keeps losing her marbles. She lost 15 on Tuesday, 85 on Wednesday, 140 on Thursday, and 210 on Friday. She originally had 500 marbles. Does she have more or fewer than 100 left?

12. Find the sum. $\frac{7}{10} + \frac{11}{100} = ?$   Change tenths to hundredths before you add.

13. Draw a model to show that $0.4 < 0.7$

14. The students of Room 403 decide to measure their hand span. Help them to organize their data into a line plot.

15. A student with the shortest hand span notices that a nearby piece of string is exactly as long as three of her hand lengths. How long is the string?

| Student | Hand Span (in.) |
|---------|-----------------|
| Toya    | 5½              |
| Kate    | 5⅛              |
| Tim     | 5⅛              |
| Joslyn  | 6               |
| Nate    | 5¼              |
| Benny   | 6¼              |
| Mario   | 5⅛              |
| Freddie | 5¼              |

| | | |
|---|---|---|
| **1.** 　　4.NBT.2 | **2.** 　　4.MD.2 | **3.** 　　4.NBT.4 |
| **4.** 　　4.NF.6 | **5.** 　　4.NF.3 | **6.** 　　4.MD.6 |
| **7.** 　　4.NF.2 $$\frac{7}{14} \bigcirc \frac{9}{14}$$ | **8.** 　　4.NBT.4 | **9.** 　　4.NBT.6 |
| **10.** 　　4.OA.1 | **11.** 　　4.OA.3 | **12.** 　　4.NF.5 |
| **13.** 　　4.NF.7 | **14 – 15.** 　　　　　4.MD.4 | |

# Lesson #129

1.  Aleah bought a computer that weighed 14 pounds, 2 ounces.  Her brother bought a laptop that weighed 3 pounds, 15 ounces.  In ounces, how much more did Aleah's computer weigh?

2.  Complete the pattern.  56, 59, 62, 65, _____, _____.  Describe the pattern.

3.  The heron flew 2,000 meters before diving in the lake for a fish.  How many kilometers did the heron fly?

4.  Find the area of the shape.  The dotted line helps to show two different rectangles.  Find the area of each rectangle, and then add them together for a total.

5.  Sissy is buying lemonade for her family at the county fair.  She has 45 tickets and each lemonade costs 7 tickets.  How many lemonades can she buy and how many tickets will be left over?

6.  Use an equivalent fraction to find the sum of $\frac{8}{10} + \frac{10}{100}$.

7.  Find the difference.  $\frac{5}{6} - \frac{2}{6} = ?$

8.  When the clock shows two o'clock, the hands form a 60° angle.  What angle do the arms form when the clock shows four o'clock?

9.  484,773 + 596,684 = ?

10. The decimal 0.07 represents _____ tenths and _____ hundredths.

11. Use a matrix model to find the product:  27 × 78 = ?

12. Mrs. Hendrix uses $\frac{1}{8}$ cup of laundry detergent each time she does a load of laundry.  She did 5 loads of laundry today.  How much detergent did Mrs. Hendrix use?  Draw a fraction model to help you solve the problem.

13. 7,943 ÷ 8 = ?

14. The famous movie star keeps her fan mail in piles sorted by month.  She decides to measure the height of each pile.  Help the movie star to organize her data into a line plot.

| Month    | Height (in.) |
|----------|--------------|
| January  | 4            |
| February | 5½           |
| March    | 4¼           |
| April    | 4            |
| May      | 5½           |
| June     | 5            |
| July     | 4¼           |
| August   | 5            |

15. What is the difference between the shortest and the tallest pile of fan mail?

| | | |
|---|---|---|
| **1.** 4.MD.2 | **2.** 4.OA.5 | **3.** 4.MD.1 |

| | | |
|---|---|---|
| **4.** 4.MD.3 | **5.** 4.OA.3 | **6.** 4.NF.5 |

| | | |
|---|---|---|
| **7.** 4.NF.3 | **8.** 4.MD.7 two o'clock    four o'clock | **9.** 4.NBT.4 |

| | | |
|---|---|---|
| **10.** 4.NF.6 | **11.** 4.NBT.5 | **12.** 4.NF.4 |

| | |
|---|---|
| **13.** 4.NBT.6 | **14 – 15.** 4.MD.4 |

# Lesson #130

1.  Round 1,376,214 to the nearest million.

2.  Find the sum. $\dfrac{9}{10} + \dfrac{19}{100} = ?$  Change tenths to hundredths before you add.

3.  Circle the shape that has perpendicular sides.  Name this shape.

4.  Missy stacked the shoeboxes 2 meters high.  How many centimeters high are the shoeboxes?

5.  Find the measure of $\angle VUT$.

6.  $375,814 + 427,266 = ?$

7.  Fill in the sign that makes the sentence true.  $0.4 \bigcirc 0.40$

8.  Choose the numbers that are multiples of both 2 and 9.

9.  Mrs. Moli put $3.25 in the parking meter outside her office. How many quarters did she put into the meter?

10.  $762 \div 8 = ?$

11.  $7,000 - 5,215 = ?$

12.  Write the sum as a mixed number.  $\dfrac{3}{4} + \dfrac{2}{4} = \dfrac{5}{4} \rightarrow \dfrac{5}{4} = \dfrac{4}{4} + \dfrac{\square}{\square} = ?$

13.  The decimal 0.3 represents _____ tenths and _____ hundredths.

14.  Fill in the sign to make this sentence true.

15.  Complete the pattern.  51, 55, 59, 63, _____, _____.  Describe the pattern.

| | | |
|---|---|---|
| **1.**    4.NBT.3 | **2.**    4.NF.5 | **3.**    4.G.2 |
| **4.**    4.MD.1 | **5.**    4.MD.6 | **6.**    4.NBT.4 |
| **7.**    4.NF.7 | **8.**    4.OA.4 <br><br> 27   36   90   54   56 | **9.**    4.MD.2 |
| **10.**    4.NBT.6 | **11.**    4.NBT.4 | **12.**    4.NF.3 <br><br> $\dfrac{4}{4} + \dfrac{\square}{\square} = \underline{\hspace{1cm}}$ |
| **13.**    4.NF.6 | **14.**    4.NF.2 <br><br> $\dfrac{4}{8} \bigcirc \dfrac{4}{5}$ | **15.**    4.OA.5 |

# Lesson #131

1.   Because of rain, the students had indoor recess 6 more times than they had the month before when they had only 4 indoor recesses.  How many indoor recesses did the students have this month?

2.   Write $\frac{8}{100}$ as a decimal.

3.   The two rays form a right angle.  What is the value of $n$?

4.   $345,772 + 736,659 = ?$

5.   Use the distributive property to multiply $24 \times 98$.

6.   The florist added 7.5 kilograms of dirt to the potted plant.  How many grams of dirt did the florist add?

7.   Ranger Jim noticed that it rained $\frac{6}{10}$ of an inch each day for 6 days in a row.  How much rain did the park have over these 6 days?  Draw a fraction model to help you solve the problem.

8.   Describe the pattern.

9.   $6,025 - 4,772 = ?$

10.  Round 197,265 to the nearest thousand.

11.  The area of a rectangular ring box is 90 cm².  The border around the ring box is 38 cm.  What is the length and width of the ring box?  Use the factor pairs of 90 to help you find the length and width of the ring box.

12.  Use an equivalent fraction to find the sum of $\frac{2}{10} + \frac{71}{100}$.

13.  Write 364,275 in expanded form.

14.  Teams of students must build the tallest tower possible using only uncooked spaghetti and marshmallows.  At the end, the height of each tower is recorded.  Help the students to organize their data into a line plot.

15.  What is the difference in height between the tallest and the second tallest tower?

| Team | Tower Height (in.) |
|------|--------------------|
| A | 14½ |
| B | 15¼ |
| C | 14¼ |
| D | 13½ |
| E | 14¼ |
| F | 13¼ |
| G | 14½ |

| 1.   4.OA.1 | 2.   4.NF.6 | 3.   4.MD.7 |
|---|---|---|
| | | |

| 4.   4.NBT.4 | 5.   4.NBT.5 | 6.   4.MD.1 |
|---|---|---|
| | | |

| 7.   4.NF.4 | 8.   4.OA.5 | 9.   4.NBT.4 |
|---|---|---|
| | | |

| 10.   4.NBT.3 | 11.   4.MD.3 | 12.   4.NF.5 |
|---|---|---|
| | | |

| 13.   4.NBT.2 | 14 – 15.   4.MD.4 |
|---|---|
| | |

# Lesson #132

1. The Eastside Knights football team defeated the Southside Cougars by 21 points on Sunday. The margin of defeat was 3 times as many points as it was when the two teams played last year. By how many points did the Knights defeat the Cougars last year? Write an equation with $n$ as the unknown and solve it.

2. Round 36,253 to the nearest hundred.

3. Which two lines are perpendicular?

4. $9,103 - 6,275 = ?$

5. Complete the pattern. 64, 61, 58, 55, _____, _____. Describe the pattern.

6. Mr. Nelson uses $\frac{4}{5}$ cup of water to water each of his 8 house plants. How many cups of water does Mr. Nelson use to water his plants? Draw a fraction model to help you solve the problem.

7. $507,544 + 267,388 = ?$

8. Which letter represents 0.94 on the number line?

9. Write the base-ten number for $600,000 + 40,000 + 3,000 + 200 + 20 + 1$.

10. Circle the right triangle.

11. Find the measure of $\angle TSR$.

12. Draw a model to show that $0.3 < 0.4$.

13. Show $\frac{4}{8}$ as the sum of unit fractions. _____ + _____ + _____ + _____ = _____

14. $\overrightarrow{QP}$ and $\overrightarrow{QR}$ are perpendicular. What is the value of $g$?

15. Fill in the sign to make this sentence true.

| 1.      4.OA.2 | 2.      4.NBT.3 | 3.      4.G.1 |
|---|---|---|
| | | |
| 4.      4.NBT.4 | 5.      4.OA.5 | 6.      4.NF.4 |
| 7.      4.NBT.4 | 8.      4.NF.6 | 9.      4.NBT.2 |
| 10.      4.G.2 | 11.      4.MD.6 | 12.      4.NF.7 |
| | | |
| 13.      4.NF.3 | 14.      4.MD.7 | 15.      4.NF.2 |
| | | $\dfrac{7}{8}\ \bigcirc\ \dfrac{3}{8}$ |

# Lesson #133

1.    Write the base-ten number for twenty-six thousand, four hundred thirty-five.

2.    Find the sum. Remember to rename fractions that have a numerator that is larger than the denominator. Write the sum as a mixed number.
$$\frac{5}{6}+\frac{3}{6}=\frac{8}{6}\rightarrow\frac{8}{6}=\frac{6}{6}+\frac{\square}{\square}=?$$

3.    $473,216 + 566,248 = ?$

4.    Tyler's old wheelchair weighed 27 pounds, 12 ounces. His new chair weighs 21 pounds. In ounces, how much lighter is Tyler's new wheelchair?

5.    Circle the shape that has parallel sides. Name this shape.

6.    Eli promised to meet his friend in 2 hours, but the wait for the rollercoaster is 60 minutes. Does Eli have enough time to ride the roller coaster before meeting his friend?

7.    Round 255,403 to the nearest hundred thousand.

8.    The decimal 0.65 represents _____ tenths and _____ hundredths.

9.    Use a protractor to draw a 75° angle. Label it $\angle OPA$.

10.    $80,000 - 36,748 = ?$

11.    If $\angle ABC$ is a straight angle, what is the value of $k$?

12.    $6,024 \div 7 = ?$

13.    William and his sister together use $\frac{3}{5}$ bag of celery in their packed lunches. How many bags of celery will their dad need to buy if they pack their lunch 4 times this week? Draw a fraction model to help you solve the problem.

14.    Samit measures the lengths of several lizards in the science room's lizard habitats. Help Samit to organize his data into a line plot.

15.    What is the difference in height between the longest lizard and the shortest?

| Lizard | Length (in.) |
|---|---|
| Skink A | 7¼ |
| Skink B | 8 |
| Skink C | 7⅛ |
| Chameleon A | 7½ |
| Chameleon B | 7½ |
| Anole A | 7⅛ |
| Anole B | 7¼ |
| Anole C | 7½ |

| | | |
|---|---|---|
| **1.** 4.NBT.2 | **2.** 4.NF.3 | **3.** 4.NBT.4 |
| **4.** 4.MD.2 | **5.** 4.G.2 | **6.** 4.MD.1 |
| **7.** 4.NBT.3 | **8.** 4.NF.6 | **9.** 4.MD.6 |
| **10.** 4.NBT.4 | **11.** 4.MD.7 | **12.** 4.NBT.6 |
| **13.** 4.NF.4 | **14 – 15.** 4.MD.4 | |

**5.** 4.G.2

**11.** 4.MD.7

$k°$
$36°$    $64°$
A      B      C

**14 – 15.** 4.MD.4

7             8

# Lesson #134

1.  $83,678 + 96,585 = ?$

2.  Write $\frac{32}{100}$ as a decimal.

3.  $4,248 \div 6 = ?$

4.  Norah practices the cello for $\frac{2}{3}$ of an hour. She practiced 4 times this week. How many hours did Norah play the cello? Draw a fraction model to help you solve the problem.

5.  The gardener gives the sunflowers 8.5 liters of water every day. How many millimeters of water do the sunflowers get each day?

6.  Complete the next shape in the sequence. Describe the pattern.

7.  Six ice cube trays can make twelve equal ice cubes each. Mary makes several glasses of ice water using $2\frac{11}{12}$ trays. Marty uses $\frac{7}{12}$ of a tray to make a smoothie. How many trays' worth of ice cubes remain? Make a visual model to help you.

8.  Fill in the sign that makes the sentence true. $0.84 \bigcirc 0.48$

9.  $3,121 - 1,756 = ?$

10. Circle the right triangle.

11. The area of a rectangular desk is 15 square feet. The border around the desk is 16 feet. What is the length and width of the desk? Use the factor pairs of 15 to help you find the length and width of the desk.

12. Fill in the sign to make this sentence true.

13. Round 568 to the nearest hundred.

14. T.J. measures the heights of his favorite action figures. Help T.J. to organize his data into a line plot.

15. If T.J. lined up the three tallest action figures end-to-end and measured them, what would be the total length?

| Action Figure | Height (in.) |
|---|---|
| Megalo-Man | 3½ |
| Scarewolf | 3⅛ |
| Turnip Face | 4 |
| Corporal Fear | 3¼ |
| Old King Bart | 3½ |
| Skip Justice | 4½ |
| Mama Mayhem | 4½ |
| The Bee Keeper | 3 |

| 1.                4.NBT.4 | 2.                4.NF.6 | 3.                4.NBT.6 |
|---|---|---|
| 4.                4.NF.4 | 5.                4.MD.1 | 6.                4.OA.5 |
| 7.                4.NF.3 | 8.                4.NF.7 | 9.                4.NBT.4 |
| 10.               4.G.2 | 11.               4.MD.3 | 12.               4.NF.2 $$\frac{5}{8} \bigcirc \frac{5}{5}$$ |
| 13.               4.NBT.3 | 14 – 15.                                            4.MD.4 | |

# Lesson #135

1.     Find the sum.  $\frac{3}{10} + \frac{4}{10} = ?$

2.     Circle the shape that has <u>only one set</u> of perpendicular sides.  Name this shape.

3.     Complete the pattern.  60, 51, 42, 33, _____, _____.  Describe the pattern.

4.     The Matthew kids each eat $\frac{3}{5}$ cup of peanuts afterschool for a snack.  If there
       are 3 kids in the Matthew family how many total cups of peanuts do they eat for
       their snack?  Draw a fraction model to help you solve the problem.

5.     135,816 + 727,905 = ?

6.     706 − 341 = ?

7.     Draw $\overrightarrow{AB}$ in the box.

8.     Draw a model to show that 0.8 > 0.3.

9.     Find the area of the shape.  The dotted line helps to show two different
       rectangles.  Find the area of each rectangle, and then add them together for a
       total.

10.    Use a protractor to draw a 100° angle.  Label it ∠SDF.

11.    Find the sum.  $\frac{8}{10} + \frac{38}{100} = ?$  Change tenths to hundredths before you add.

12.    Which letter represents 0.12
       on the number line?

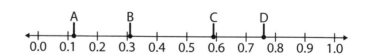

13.    835 ÷ 4 = ?

14.    Greg went into the bookstore with $11.24 and came out with $1.23.  How much
       money did Greg spend in the store?

15.    The cinema showed an 8 minute cartoon before the movie started.  How many
       seconds did the cartoon last?

| | | |
|---|---|---|
| **1.** 4.NF.3 | **2.** 4.G.2 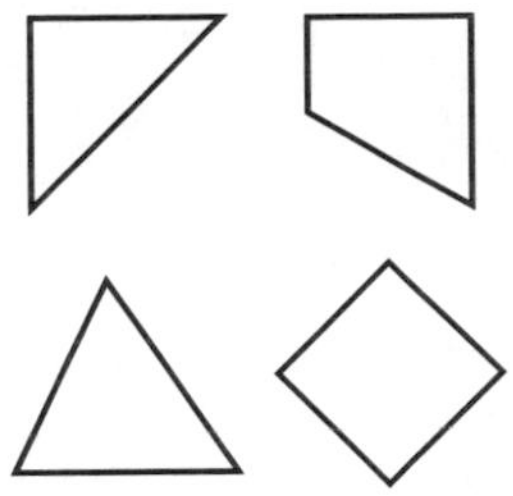 | **3.** 4.OA.5 |
| **4.** 4.NF.4 | **5.** 4.NBT.4 | **6.** 4.NBT.4 |
| **7.** 4.G.1 | **8.** 4.NF.7 | **9.** 4.MD.3 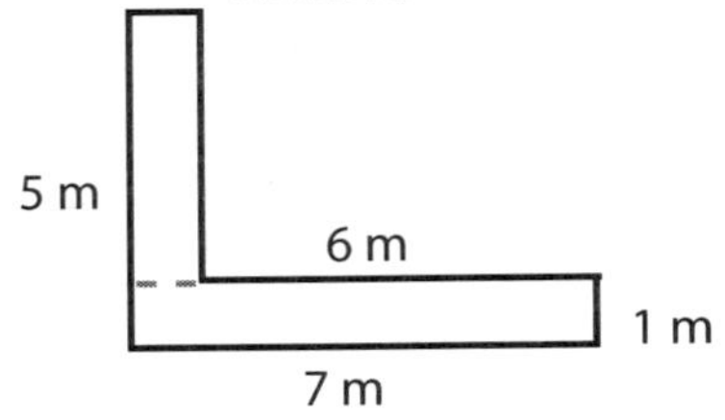  |
| **10.** 4.MD.6 | **11.** 4.NF.5 | **12.** 4.NF.6 |
| **13.** 4.NBT.6 | **14.** 4.MD.2 | **15.** 4.MD.1 |

# Lesson #136

1.      $502 - 177 = ?$

2.      Mr. Tyler runs $\frac{6}{10}$ of a mile for exercise.  If Mr. Tyler runs 5 times this week, how many miles does he run?  Draw a fraction model to help you solve the problem.

3.      Fill in the sign to make this sentence true.

4.      Joyce bunted the softball 66 inches up the left base line.  How many feet did Joyce bunt the ball?

5.      The decimal 0.01 represents _____ tenths and _____ hundredths.

6.      Circle the right triangle.

7.      Write the sum as a mixed number.  $\frac{7}{8} + \frac{7}{8} = \frac{14}{8} \rightarrow \frac{14}{8} = \frac{8}{8} + \frac{\square}{\square} = ?$

8.      The area of a rectangular room is 56 ft².  The border around the room is 30 feet.  What is the length and width of the room?  Use the factor pairs of 56 to help you find the length and width of the room.

9.      Find the measure of $\angle YXW$.

10.     Round 86,245 to the nearest hundred.

11.     Use a matrix model to find the product:   $18 \times 45 = ?$

12.     The two rays form a right angle.  What is the value of $y$?

13.     $71,688 + 89,213 = ?$

14.     The science class keeps several pet mice.  They decide to record the length of each mouse.  Help the class to organize their data into a line plot.

15.     One student lines up the three longest mice end-to-end.  The mice politely stand there to be measured.  What is the total length of the three mice?

| Mouse | Length (in.) |
|---|---|
| Sally | 4 ½ |
| Sandy | 5 ½ |
| Max | 4 |
| Frank | 5 |
| Diane | 4¼ |
| Tom | 6½ |
| Chris | 5¼ |
| Michelle | 6 |

| | | |
|---|---|---|
| **1.** 4.NBT.4 | **2.** 4.NF.4 | **3.** 4.NF.2 $$\frac{14}{17} \bigcirc \frac{8}{17}$$ |
| **4.** 4.MD.1 | **5.** 4.NF.6 | **6.** 4.G.2 |
| **7.** 4.NF.3 $$\frac{8}{8} + \frac{\square}{\square} = \underline{\hspace{1cm}}$$ | **8.** 4.MD.3 | **9.** 4.MD.6 |
| **10.** 4.NBT.3 | **11.** 4.NBT.5 | **12.** 4.MD.7 |
| **13.** 4.NBT.4 | **14 – 15.** 4.MD.4 | |

# Lesson #137

1.  Circle the shape that has <u>only one</u> set of parallel sides.  What do we call this shape?

2.  Fill in the sign that makes the sentence true.   0.02 ◯ 0.2

3.  34,866 + 25,755 = ?

4.  Devon bought a bottle of water from the vending machine. The water cost $1.20.  He only put dimes in the machine. How many dimes did he use?

5.  Write $\frac{9}{10}$ as a decimal.

6.  Draw an obtuse angle.  Label it *CAR*.

7.  621 − 366 = ?

8.  Write 26,413 using words.

9.  Find the measure of ∠*JIH*.

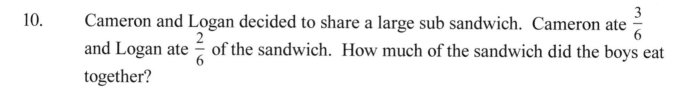

10. Cameron and Logan decided to share a large sub sandwich.  Cameron ate $\frac{3}{6}$ and Logan ate $\frac{2}{6}$ of the sandwich.  How much of the sandwich did the boys eat together?

11. If ∠*DEF* is a straight angle, what is the value of *z*?

12. 4,509 ÷ 3 = ?

13. Round 325,461 to the nearest ten thousand.

14. Jennie recorded the amount of rainfall for each day that it rained during the first two weeks of April. Help Jennie to organize her data into a line plot.

15. What was the total amount of rainfall for the days Jennie recorded?

| Day | Rainfall(in.) |
|---|---|
| 1 | ½ |
| 2 | ½ |
| 3 | 1 |
| 4 | 2 |
| 5 | ½ |
| 6 | 1½ |
| 7 | 2½ |
| 8 | 1 |

| **1.** 4.G.2 | **2.** 4.NF.7 | **3.** 4.NBT.4 |
|---|---|---|
| **4.** 4.MD.2 | **5.** 4.NF.6 | **6.** 4.G.1 |
| **7.** 4.NBT.4 | **8.** 4.NBT.2 | **9.** 4.MD.6 |
| **10.** 4.NF.3 | **11.** 4.MD.7 | **12.** 4.NBT.6 |
| **13.** 4.NBT.3 | **14 – 15.** 4.MD.4 | |

# Lesson #138

1.    Paula puts $\frac{4}{5}$ cup of nuts in each loaf of nut bread.  If she makes 5 loaves of bread, how many cups of nuts does Paula use?  Draw a fraction model to help you solve the problem.

2.    Draw a model to show that $0.1 < 0.2$.

3.    $90,000 - 27,774 = ?$

4.    The dolphin dived 144 inches to the bottom of the pool.  How many yards did the dolphin dive?

5.    Find the difference.  $\frac{8}{12} - \frac{3}{12} = ?$

6.    Which angles are acute?

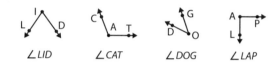

∠LID          ∠CAT          ∠DOG          ∠LAP

7.    $286,777 + 434,916 = ?$

8.    Fill in the sign to make this sentence true.

9.    Write the expanded form of the number 93,476.

10.   Which letter represents 0.44 on the number line?

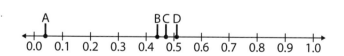

11.   $547 \div 6 = ?$

12.   Use a protractor to draw a 130° angle.  Label it ∠GHJ.

13.   Complete the next shape in the sequence.
      Describe the pattern.

14.   Circle the right triangle.

15.   Round 436 to the nearest hundred.

| 1.     4.NF.4 | 2.     4.NF.7 | 3.     4.NBT.4 |
|---|---|---|
| 4.     4.MD.1 | 5.     4.NF.3 | 6.     4.G.1 |
| 7.     4.NBT.4 | 8.     4.NF.2 $$\frac{1}{2} \bigcirc \frac{1}{3}$$ | 9.     4.NBT.2 |
| 10.     4.NF.6 | 11.     4.NBT.6 | 12.     4.MD.6 |
| 13.     4.OA.5 | 14.     4.G.2 | 15.     4.NBT.3 |

# Lesson #139

1. Stella collected 8 times as many sand dollars as starfish. She collected 7 starfish. How many sand dollars did Stella collect?

2. $5,445 \div 9 = ?$

3. $419,286 \bigcirc 419,862$

4. $48,276 + 37,145 = ?$

5. Use the distributive property to multiply $67 \times 37$.

6. Use an equivalent fraction to find the sum of $\dfrac{6}{10} + \dfrac{28}{100}$.

7. Find the area of the shape. The dotted line helps to show two different rectangles. Find the area of each rectangle, and then add them together for a total.

8. Circle the shape that has perpendicular sides. What do we call this shape?

9. Write the sum as a mixed number. $\dfrac{8}{12} + \dfrac{6}{12} = \dfrac{14}{12} \rightarrow \dfrac{14}{12} = \dfrac{12}{12} + \dfrac{\square}{\square} = ?$

10. Fill in the sign that makes the sentence true. $0.35 \bigcirc 0.3$

11. Which shows $\angle ABC$?  A)  B)  C)  D)

12. The uphill mountain trail is 7 kilometers. How many meters is that?

13. The decimal 0.5 represents _____ tenths and _____ hundredths.

14. Joe went to the costume shop to buy props for the school play. He spent $11.43 on a wig, $2.40 on a toy phone, and $9.32 on a chair. How much money did Joe spend at the costume shop?

15. If Mr. Wright gave each of the 8 kids in his music class $\dfrac{1}{5}$ package of cookies, how many packages of cookies would he need? Between what two whole numbers does your answer lie?

| | | |
|---|---|---|
| **1.**　　4.OA.1 | **2.**　　4.NBT.6 | **3.**　　4.NBT.2 |
| **4.**　　4.NBT.4 | **5.**　　4.NBT.5 | **6.**　　4.NF.5 |
| **7.**　　4.MD.3 <br><br> 6 cm ⎸ 5 cm <br> 3 cm <br> 9 cm | **8.**　　4.G.2 | **9.**　　4.NF.3 <br><br> $\dfrac{12}{12} + \dfrac{\square}{\square} = $ ___ |
| **10.**　　4.NF.7 | **11.**　　4.G.1 | **12.**　　4.MD.1 |
| **13.**　　4.NF.6 | **14.**　　4.MD.2 | **15.**　　4.NF.4 |

# Lesson #140

1.   Round 336,205 to the nearest ten thousand.

2.   $8,525 \div 5 = ?$

3.   Find the measure of $\angle IHG$.

4.   $16,204 - 9,198 = ?$

5.   Complete the pattern. 8, 15, 22, _____, _____, _____. Describe the pattern.

6.   The decimal 0.97 represents _____ tenths and _____ hundredths.

7.   The fountain in the center of town holds 39 liters of water. If 850 milliliters evaporate, how many milliliters of water will be left in the fountain?

8.   Circle the right triangle.

9.   The two rays form a right angle. What is the value of $n$?

10.   Use the distributive property to multiply $7,671 \times 6$.

11.   Write the name of the obtuse angle in the answer box.

$\angle LID$    $\angle CAT$    $\angle DOG$    $\angle LAP$

12.   The Candid Candy Store sold 167 candies on Monday, 116 candies on Tuesday, 143 candies on Wednesday, and 134 candies on Thursday. Did they sell more or less than 600 candies?

13.   $88,415 + 79,385 = ?$

14.   Fill in the sign to make this sentence true.

15.   Use a matrix model to find the product: $71 \times 32 = ?$

| | | |
|---|---|---|
| **1.**      4.NBT.3 | **2.**      4.NBT.6 | **3.**      4.MD.6 |
| **4.**      4.NBT.4 | **5.**      4.OA.5 | **6.**      4.NF.6 |
| **7.**      4.MD.2 | **8.**      4.G.2 | **9.**      4.MD.7 |
| **10.**      4.NBT.5 | **11.**      4.G.1 | **12.**      4.OA.3 |
| **13.**      4.NBT.4 | **14.**      4.NF.2 $$\frac{5}{12} \bigcirc \frac{8}{12}$$ | **15.**      4.NBT.5 |

# Common Core Mathematics 4

# Help Pages

# Help Pages

## Vocabulary

**Acute angle** — an angle measuring less than 90°

**Area** — the amount of space within a polygon; area is always measured in square units  (feet², meters²,...)

**Congruent** — figures with the same shape and the same size

**Decimal** — a number that contains a decimal point; any whole number or fraction can be written as a decimal    **Example:** $\frac{1}{10}$ = 0.10

**Denominator** — the bottom number of a fraction    **Example:** $\frac{1}{4}$; the denominator is 4.

**Difference** — the result or answer to a subtraction problem    **Example:** The difference of 5 and 1 is 4.

**Equivalent fractions** — fractions with different names but equal value

**Factor** — all of the whole numbers that can be divided exactly into a given number
The factors of 6 are 1 and 6, 2 and 3.

**Fraction** — a part of a whole    **Example:**    This box has 4 parts. 1 part is shaded.  $\frac{1}{4}$ is shaded.

**Line** — has no endpoints, goes forever in two directions     A     B

**Line of symmetry** — a line along which a figure can be folded so that the two halves match exactly

**Line segment** – line with end points   Say, "line segment MN" or "line segment NM."       M•———•N

**Mixed number** — the sum of a whole number and a fraction    **Example:** $5\frac{3}{4}$

**Multiple** — the product of two whole numbers
When you skip count by twos, you say the multiples of two.

**Numerator** — the top number of a fraction    **Example:** $\frac{1}{4}$; the numerator is 1.

**Obtuse angle** — an angle measuring more than 90°

**Parallel lines** — two lines that never intersect and are always the same distance apart

Q      R
S      T

**Perimeter** — the distance around the outside of a polygon

**Perpendicular lines** — lines that intersect and form a right angle (90°)

This square means the angle is 90°.

**Point** — has no length or width; named with a capital letter   • A

# Help Pages

## Vocabulary

| | |
|---|---|
| **Product** — the result or answer to a multiplication problem | **Example**: The product of 5 and 3 is 15. |
| **Quotient** — the result or answer to a division problem | **Example**: The quotient of 8 and 2 is 4. |
| **Ray** — a line that goes on in one direction    Say, "ray FG."    F ●———————→ G | |
| **Right angle** — an angle measuring exactly 90° | |
| **Sum** — the result or answer to an addition problem | **Example**: The sum of 5 and 2 is 7. |
| **Unit fraction** — a fraction with a numerator of 1 | |

### Geometry — Polygons — Two-dimensional

| Number of Sides | Name | Number of Sides | Name |
|---|---|---|---|
| 3 △ | Triangle | 5 ⬠ | Pentagon |
| 4 ▢ ▭ | Quadrilateral | 6 ⬡ | Hexagon |

### Measurement — Equivalent Units

| Volume | Distance |
|---|---|
| 1 liter (L) = 1,000 milliliters (mL) | 1 foot (ft) = 12 inches (in.) |
| **Weight** | 1 yard (yd) = 3 feet (ft) = 36 inches (in.) |
| 1 kilogram (kg) = 1,000 grams (g) | 1 meter (m) = 100 centimeters (cm) |
| 1 pound (lb) = 16 ounces (oz) | 1 kilometer (km) = 1,000 meters (m) |
| **Time** | |
| 1 hour (hr) = 60 minutes (min) | 1 minute (min) = 60 seconds (sec) |

## Place Value

### Whole Numbers

| 1, | 2 | 7 | 1, | 4 | 0 | 5 |
|---|---|---|---|---|---|---|
| millions | hundred thousands | ten thousands | thousands | hundreds | tens | ones |

The number above is read: one million, two hundred seventy-one thousand, four hundred five.

# Help Pages

| Decimals |
| --- |

$$1 \quad 7 \quad 8 \quad . \quad 6 \quad 4$$

hundreds    tens    ones    *decimal point* ⇧    tenths    hundredths

The number above is read: one hundred seventy-eight and sixty-four hundredths.

| Rounding Numbers Using Place Value |
| --- |

1. Identify the greatest place value: What is the greatest place value in the number?

   Thousands **3**,421    This number is between 3,000 and 4,000.

   Hundreds **7**89    This number is between 700 and 800.

   Tens **2**3    This number is between 20 and 30.

2. Round to that place value. Is the number closer to _____ or _____?

   Is 3,421 closer to 3,000 or 4,000?

   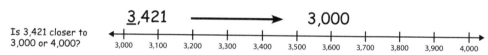

   Is 789 closer to 700 or 800?

   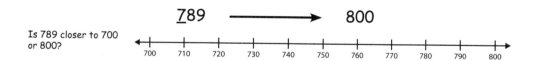

   Is 23 closer to 20 or 30?

   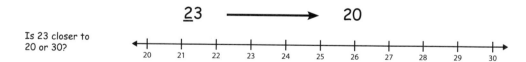

3. If the number is right in the middle, round up.

   8,500 ⟶ 9,000
   450 ⟶ 500
   65 ⟶ 70

4. Round 48,695 to the nearest thousand.
   - What number is in the thousands place? (8)
   - 48,695 is between 48,000 and 49,000.
   - 48,695 is closer to 49,000 than it is to 48,000.

5. Round 441 to the nearest ten.
   - What number is in the tens place? (4)
   - 441 is between 440 and 450.
   - 441 is closer to 440 than it is to 450.

# Help Pages

## Solved Examples

### Whole Numbers - Rounding to Any Place Value

When we **round numbers**, we are estimating them. This means we focus on a particular place value and decide if that digit is closer to the next highest number (round up) or to the next lower number (keep the same). It might be helpful to look at the place value chart on the previous page.

**Example:** Round 4,826 to the hundreds place.

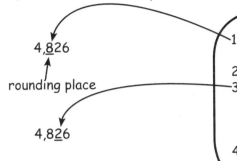

4,8<u>2</u>6

rounding place

4,8<u>2</u>6

1. Identify the place that you want to round to. What number is in that place? (8)
2. Look at the digit to its right.
3. If this digit is 5 or greater, increase the number in the rounding place by 1. (round up) If the digit is less than 5, keep the number in the rounding place the same.
4. Replace all digits to the right of the rounding place with zeros.

Since 2 is less than 5, the rounding place <u>stays the same.</u>

4,800

**Example**: Round 27,934 to the thousands place.

2<u>7</u>,934  ⟶  7 is in the rounding place.

27,<u>9</u>34  ⟶  9 is greater than 5, so the rounding place will go up by 1.

28,000  ⟶  The digits to the right of the rounding place are changed to zeros.

### Whole Numbers - Addition and Subtraction

**When adding or subtracting whole numbers**, first the numbers must be lined up on the right. Starting with the ones place, add (or subtract) the numbers; when adding, if the answer has 2 digits, write the ones digit and regroup the tens digit (for subtraction, it may also be necessary to regroup first). Then, add (or subtract) the numbers in the tens place. Continue with the hundreds, etc.

Look at these examples of addition.

**Examples**: Find the sum of 314 and 12.                        Add 6,478 and 1,843.

```
  314
+  12
─────
  326
```

1. Line up the numbers on the right.
2. Beginning with the ones place, add. Regroup if necessary.
3. Repeat with the tens place.
4. Continue this process with the hundreds place, etc.

```
  ¹ ¹ ¹
  6,478
+ 1,843
──────
  8,321
```

# Help Pages

## Solved Examples

---

**Whole Numbers  -  Addition and Subtraction (continued)**

---

Use the following examples of subtraction to help you.

**Example:**   Subtract 37 from 93.

$$
\begin{array}{r}
{\scriptstyle 8\ \ 13} \\
\not{9}\ \not{3} \\
-\ 3\ 7 \\
\hline
5\ 6
\end{array}
$$

1. Begin with the ones place.  Check to see if you need to regroup.  Since 7 is larger than 3, you must regroup to 8 tens and 13 ones.

2. Now look at the tens place.  Since 3 is less than 8, you do not need to regroup.

3. Subtract each place value beginning with the ones.

---

**Example:** Find the difference of 4,125 and 2,033.

$$
\begin{array}{r}
{\scriptstyle 0\ \ 12} \\
4,\not{1}\not{2}5 \\
-\ 2,0\ 3\ 3 \\
\hline
2,0\ 9\ 2
\end{array}
$$

1. Begin with the ones place.  Check to see if you need to regroup.  Since 3 is less than 5, you do not need to regroup.

2. Now look at the tens place.  Check to see if you need to regroup.  Since 3 is larger than 2, you must regroup to 0 hundreds and 12 tens.

3. Now look at the thousands place.  Since 2 is less than 4, you are ready to subtract.

4. Subtract each place value beginning with the ones.

---

Sometimes when doing subtraction, you must **subtract from zero**.  This always requires regrouping. Use the examples below to help you.

**Examples:**  Subtract 2,361 from 5,000.

$$
\begin{array}{r}
{\scriptstyle 4\ \ 10\ \ 10\ \ 10} \\
{\scriptstyle \ \ \ 9\ \ \ 9} \\
\not{5},\not{0}\ \not{0}\ \not{0} \\
-\ 2,\ 3\ 6\ 1 \\
\hline
2,\ 6\ 3\ 9
\end{array}
$$

1. Begin with the ones place.  Since 1 is larger than 0, you must regroup.  You must continue to the thousands place, and then begin regrouping.

2. Regroup the thousands place to 4 thousands and 10 hundreds.

3. Next regroup the hundreds place to 9 hundreds and 10 tens.

4. Then, regroup the tens place to 9 tens and 10 ones.

5. Finally, subtract each place value beginning with the ones.

Find the difference between 600 and 238.

$$
\begin{array}{r}
{\scriptstyle 5\ \ 10\ \ 10} \\
{\scriptstyle \ \ \ 9} \\
\not{6}\ \not{0}\ \not{0} \\
-\ 2\ 3\ 8 \\
\hline
3\ 6\ 2
\end{array}
$$

# Help Pages

## Whole Numbers - Multiplication Table of Basic Facts

It is very important that you memorize your **multiplication facts**. This table will help you as you memorize them!

To use this table, choose a number in the top gray box and multiply it by a number in the left gray box. Follow both with your fingers (one down and one across) until they meet. The number in that box is the product.

An example is shown for you:  $2 \times 3 = 6$

| x | 0 | 1 | 2 | 3 | 4 | 5 | 6 | 7 | 8 | 9 | 10 |
|---|---|---|---|---|---|---|---|---|---|---|----|
| 0 | 0 | 0 | 0 | 0 | 0 | 0 | 0 | 0 | 0 | 0 | 0 |
| 1 | 0 | 1 | 2 | 3 | 4 | 5 | 6 | 7 | 8 | 9 | 10 |
| 2 | 0 | 2 | 4 | 6 | 8 | 10 | 12 | 14 | 16 | 18 | 20 |
| 3 | 0 | 3 | 6 | 9 | 12 | 15 | 18 | 21 | 24 | 27 | 30 |
| 4 | 0 | 4 | 8 | 12 | 16 | 20 | 24 | 28 | 32 | 36 | 40 |
| 5 | 0 | 5 | 10 | 15 | 20 | 25 | 30 | 35 | 40 | 45 | 50 |
| 6 | 0 | 6 | 12 | 18 | 24 | 30 | 36 | 42 | 48 | 54 | 60 |
| 7 | 0 | 7 | 14 | 21 | 28 | 35 | 42 | 49 | 56 | 63 | 70 |
| 8 | 0 | 8 | 16 | 24 | 32 | 40 | 48 | 56 | 64 | 72 | 80 |
| 9 | 0 | 9 | 18 | 27 | 36 | 45 | 54 | 63 | 72 | 81 | 90 |
| 10 | 0 | 10 | 20 | 30 | 40 | 50 | 60 | 70 | 80 | 90 | 100 |

# Help Pages

## Solved Examples

### Whole Numbers - Multiplication

**When multiplying multi-digit whole numbers,** it is important to know your multiplication facts. Follow the steps and the examples below.

Here is a way to multiply a four-digit whole number by a one-digit whole number.

Use the **distributive property** to multiply 3,514 x 3.

Multiply 3 by all the values in 3,514 (3,000 + 500 + 10 + 4).

Add all the partial products to get one final product.

$$\begin{array}{r} \overset{1\quad 1}{3,514} \\ \times\ \ 3 \\ \hline 10,542 \end{array}$$

3 × 4 = 12 ones or 1 ten and 2 ones.

3 × 10 = 3 tens + 1 ten (regrouped) or 4 tens.

3 × 500 = 15 hundreds or 1 thousand and 5 hundreds.

3 × 3,000 = 9 thousands + 1 thousand (regrouped) or 10 thousands.

(3,000 x 3) + (500 x 3) + (10 x 3) + (4 x 3) = 9,000 + 1,500 + 30 + 12 = 10,542

Here are two ways to multiply two two-digit numbers.

Use the **distributive property** to multiply 36 x 12.

Multiply the two addends of 36 (30 + 6) by the two addends of 12 (10 + 2).

Then, add all the partial products to get one final product.

$$\begin{array}{r} 36 \\ \times\ 12 \\ \hline 432 \end{array}$$

2 x 6 = 12

2 x 30 = 60

10 x 6 = 60

10 x 30 = 300

(30 x 10) + (30 x 2) + (6 x 10) + (6 x 2) = 300 + 60 + 60 + 12 = 432

Use the **matrix model** to multipy 48 x 31.

The model shows the four parts needed to arrive at the final product.

Place the expanded form of each two-digit number on the outside edge of the boxes as shown.

Write the partial products in each box. The sum of the four partial products is 1,488.

Notice the two different addition problems that serve as a way to check your accuracy.

|      | 40    | 8   |       |
|------|-------|-----|-------|
| 30   | 1,200 | 240 | 1,440 |
| 1    | 40    | 8   | + 48  |
|      | 1,240 | 248 | 1,488 |

# Help Pages

## Solved Examples

### Factors and Multiples

In the basic fact 2 × 3 = 6, 2 and 3 are called **factors**, and the **product** is 6.

To name all the **factor pairs** of 20, think of every factor pair that will result in a product of 20 (1 × 20, 2 × 10, 4 × 5). Then list those factors from smallest to largest (1, 2, 4, 5, 10, and 20).

A **multiple** is the product of two whole numbers. When you skip count by twos, you say the multiples of two. The first five multiples of 2 are 2, 4, 6, 8, and 10.

### Prime and Composite

**Prime Numbers:** A prime number is a number greater than 1 that has only two factors, 1 and itself. 2 and 7 are prime numbers: 2 × 1 = 2; 7 × 1 = 7.

**Composite Numbers:** A composite number has more than two factors. 12 is a composite number with 6 factors: 1, 2, 3, 4, 6, 12.

### Division – Place value model

**Example:** Solve. 8,524 ÷ 4

1. Expand the dividend and write it in the place value model. 8,524 = 8,000 + 500 + 20 + 4 The dotted box is for a remainder.

2. Put the divisor in front of the model.   4 | 8,000 | 500 | 20 | 4 | ⋯

3. Divide 4 into each place value.

- How many 4s are in 8,000? (2,000 × 4 = 8,000)

  2,000
  4 | 8,000 | 500 | 20 | 4 | ⋯

- How many 4s are in 500? (125 × 4 = 500)

  2,000   125
  4 | 8,000 | 500 | 20 | 4 | ⋯

- How many 4s are in 20? (5 × 4 = 20)

  2,000   125   5
  4 | 8,000 | 500 | 20 | 4 | ⋯

- How many 4s are in 4? (1 × 4 = 4)

  2,000   125   5   1
  4 | 8,000 | 500 | 20 | 4 | ⋯

4. Record the partial quotients.
5. Add the numbers in step 4 to find the final quotient.

   2,000
   125
   5
   + 1
   ———
   2,131

8,524 ÷ 4 = 2,131. There is no remainder.

# Help Pages

## Solved Examples

**Division - Whole Numbers**

**Example:** Divide 9,603 by 4.

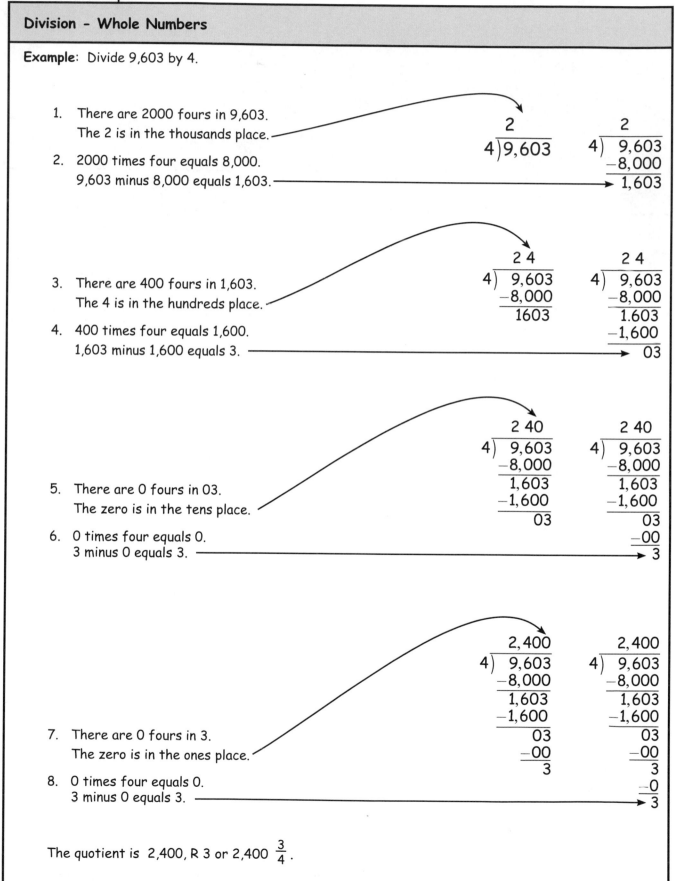

1. There are 2000 fours in 9,603.
   The 2 is in the thousands place.

2. 2000 times four equals 8,000.
   9,603 minus 8,000 equals 1,603.

3. There are 400 fours in 1,603.
   The 4 is in the hundreds place.

4. 400 times four equals 1,600.
   1,603 minus 1,600 equals 3.

5. There are 0 fours in 03.
   The zero is in the tens place.

6. 0 times four equals 0.
   3 minus 0 equals 3.

7. There are 0 fours in 3.
   The zero is in the ones place.

8. 0 times four equals 0.
   3 minus 0 equals 3.

The quotient is 2,400, R 3 or 2,400 $\frac{3}{4}$.

# Help Pages

## Solved Examples

### Fractions - Equivalent Fractions

**Equivalent Fractions** are 2 fractions that are equal to each other. Usually you will be finding a missing numerator or denominator.

**Example:** Find a fraction that is equivalent to $\frac{4}{5}$ and has a denominator of 35.

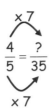

1. Ask yourself, "What did I do to 5 to get 35?" (Multiplied by 7.)
2. Whatever you did in the denominator, you also must do in the numerator. $4 \times 7 = 28$    The missing numerator is 28.

So, $\frac{4}{5}$ is equivalent to $\frac{28}{35}$.

**Example:** Find a fraction that is equivalent to $\frac{4}{5}$ and has a numerator of 24.

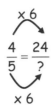

1. Ask yourself, "What did I do to 4 to get 24?" (Multiplied by 6.)
2. Whatever you did in the numerator, you also must do in the denominator. $5 \times 6 = 30$  The missing denominator is 30.

So, $\frac{4}{5}$ is equivalent to $\frac{24}{30}$.

### Fractions - Comparing Fractions

When you are given a visual model like a number line to compare two fractions, the fraction that is farthest to the right on the number line is greater.

**Example:** Choose the sign that makes this sentence true. ( < > = )    $\frac{1}{2} \bigcirc \frac{7}{8}$

Find the fractions on each number line. The fraction that is farthest to the right is greater.

$$\frac{1}{2} < \frac{7}{8}$$

When you do not have a number line, think about what you already know.

**Example:** Choose the sign that makes this sentence true.    $\frac{3}{8} \bigcirc \frac{1}{2}$

Think about this: Half of 8 is 4, so $\frac{4}{8}$ equals $\frac{1}{2}$. Which has more eighths, $\frac{3}{8}$ or $\frac{4}{8}$? That will help you know which is greater.

$$\frac{3}{8} < \frac{1}{2}$$

**Example:** Choose the sign that makes this sentence true. ( < > = )    $\frac{5}{6} \bigcirc \frac{2}{6}$

To compare fractions with like denominators, simply compare the numerators.

$$\frac{5}{6} > \frac{2}{6} \text{, because } 5 > 2.$$

# Help Pages

## Solved Examples

### Fractions (continued)

Compare the unit fractions at the right. Notice that the larger the denominator, the smaller the unit is.

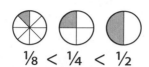

$\frac{1}{8} < \frac{1}{4} < \frac{1}{2}$

**Example:** Choose the sign that makes this sentence true. ( < > = )    $\frac{4}{5} \bigcirc \frac{4}{10}$

To compare fractions with like numerators, remember that the larger the denominator, the smaller the unit is.

$\frac{4}{5} > \frac{4}{10}$    This is true because fifths are larger units than tenths are.

### Fractions - Decomposing a Fraction or Mixed Number

Decompose (break down into smaller parts) the fraction $\frac{6}{7}$. Show the sum in two different ways.
Here's an example:

$$\frac{6}{7} = \frac{5}{7} + \frac{1}{7} \qquad \frac{6}{7} = \frac{3}{7} + \frac{3}{7}$$

Decompose (break down into smaller parts) the mixed number $2\frac{5}{12}$. Show the sum in two different ways.
Here's an example:

$$\frac{29}{12} = 1 + 1 + \frac{5}{12} \qquad \frac{29}{12} = \frac{12}{12} + \frac{12}{12} + \frac{2}{12} + \frac{3}{12}$$

### Fractions Models for Multiplication

**Example:** Use the fraction model to solve $4 \times \frac{2}{3}$. This fraction model shows $4 \times \frac{2}{3}$.

The first model shows that four groups of $\frac{2}{3}$ is $\frac{8}{3}$.

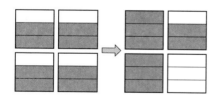

The second model shows that $\frac{8}{3}$ is equal to the mixed number $2\frac{2}{3}$.

### Decimals

All fractions with denominators of 10 and 100 can be written as decimals. The decimal 0.50 can be described as 5 tenths or 50 hundredths.

$$\frac{5}{10} = 0.5$$

$$\frac{50}{100} = 0.50$$

The fraction and decimal below can be decomposed (broken down) into $0.5 \left(\frac{5}{10}\right) + 0.03 \left(\frac{3}{100}\right)$.

$$\frac{53}{100} = 0.53$$

# Help Pages

## Solved Examples

### Rectangles – Perimeter

A rectangle has 2 pairs of parallel sides.  The distance around the outside of a rectangle is the perimeter.  To find the perimeter of a rectangle, add the lengths of the sides:
**Example:**

$$10 + 4 + 10 + 4 = 28 \text{ in.}$$
or
$$2 (10 + 4) = 2 \times 14 = 28 \text{ in.}$$
or
$$(2 \times 10) + (2 \times 4) = 28 \text{ in.}$$

4 in.

10 in.   10 in.

4 in.

### Rectangles – Area

Area is the number of square units within any 2-dimensional shape.

A rectangle has side lengths called length and width.  To find the area of a rectangle, multiply the length by the width ($l \times w$).

In the example, $10 \times 4 = 40$ in.$^2$

4 in.

10 in.   10 in.

4 in.

Remember to label your answer in square units.  Examples:
square inches: in.$^2$
square feet: ft$^2$
square yards: yd$^2$
square miles: mi$^2$
square centimeters: cm$^2$
square meters: m$^2$

If the area is known, but the length or width is missing, use division to find the missing measurement.

**Example:** The area of a rectangle is 70 square inches.  The length of one of the sides is 10 inches.  Find the width.  Label the answer.

If $A = l \times w$, then $A \div w = l$ and $A \div l = w$.  Show:  $70 \div 10 = 7$.

The width is 7 inches.

### Rectangles – Find the Length and Width

**Example:** The area of a rectangular sandbox is 18 m$^2$.  The border around the sandbox is 18 m.  What are the length and width of the sandbox?  Use the factor pairs of 18 to help you find the area of the sandbox first.

In this example, the area and perimeter are clues to the size of the length and width.

The area is 18 m$^2$. The factor pairs of 18 are $1 \times 18$, $2 \times 9$, and $3 \times 6$. One of those pairs can be the length and width of a rectangle that has a perimeter of 18 m.  Use the guess and check strategy to find the right pair.

$$1 + 1 + 18 + 18 \neq 18$$
$$2 + 2 + 9 + 9 \neq 18$$
$$3 + 3 + 6 + 6 = 18$$

The length of the rectangle is 6 m and the width is 3 m.

# Help Pages

## Solved Examples

---

### Rectangles – Find the Area of Irregular Shapes

**Example:** Find the area of the shape. The dotted line helps to show two different rectangles. Find the area of each rectangle, and then add them together for a total.

① This irregular shape is made of a large rectangle and a smaller one.

② The side lengths of the larger rectangle are clear. The length is 10 cm and the width is 4 cm.

③ The small rectangle has a side length of 1 cm, but the other side is not labeled. However, notice that the top side length is 12 cm and the bottom one is 10 cm. By subtracting 10 from 12, you can see that the missing length is 2 cm. Use that number to calculate the smaller area.

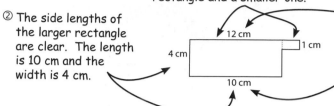

(4 x 10) large rectangle + (2 x 1) small rectangle = 40 + 2 = 42 cm²

The total area of the shape is 42 cm².

---

### Interpreting Data – Line Plots

On a line plot you can quickly see data. It may be spread out or close together.

**Example:**

Gary recorded the heights of several students from different grades. Help Gary to organize his data into a line plot.

① To make a line plot, give the line plot a title.

| Student | Height (ft.) |
|---------|--------------|
| Kelly | 4 |
| Jerome | 3¼ |
| Ming | 4½ |
| D'Andre | 3½ |
| Kyle | 3¼ |
| Maria | 4¼ |
| Hector | 4 |
| Devin | 3½ |

③ Draw a number line on the grid paper near the bottom. The number line should begin with the lowest value you found.

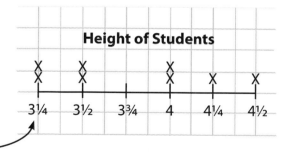

② Find the greatest value and the lowest value in the set of data.

④ The length of your line should include space to mark from your lowest to your greatest value.

⑤ For each piece of data, draw an "x" above the matching value. An "x" on the line plot will take the place of each number from the data chart. No student names are needed.

What is the difference in height between the second tallest student and the shortest student?

The second tallest student is $4\frac{1}{4}$ ft. The shortest student is $3\frac{1}{4}$ ft.

$$4\frac{1}{4} - 3\frac{1}{4} = 1 \text{ ft}$$

The difference between them is 1 foot.

# Help Pages

## Solved Examples

### Geometric Measurement – Angles

$\angle ABC$ is a **right angle** that measures exactly 90°.

$\angle DEF$ is an **acute angle**. An acute angle measures less than 90°.

$\angle XYZ$ is an **obtuse angle**. An obtuse angle measures greater than 90° and less than 180°.

### Geometric Measurement – Find the Measure of an Angle

To **find the measure of an angle**, a protractor is used.

The symbol for angle is $\angle$. On the diagram, $\angle AOE$ has a measure less than 90°, so it is acute.

With the center of the protractor on the vertex of the angle (where the 2 rays meet), place one ray ($\overline{OA}$) on one of the "0" lines. Look at the number that the other ray ($\overline{OE}$) passes through. Since the angle is acute, use the lower set of numbers. Since $\overline{OE}$ is halfway between the 40 and the 50, the measure of $\angle AOE$ is 45°. (If it were an obtuse angle, the higher set of numbers would be used.)

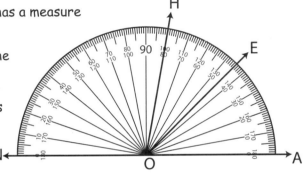

Look at $\angle NOH$ It is an obtuse angle, so the higher set of numbers will be used. Notice that $\overline{ON}$ is on the "0" line. $\overline{OH}$ passes through the 100 mark. So the measure of $\angle NOH$ is 100°.

### Geometric Measurement – Find the Missing Angle Measure

**Example:** If $\angle DEF$ is a right angle (90°), what is the measure of $n$?

In this example, $65 + n = 90$. To find the missing angle measure $n$, subtract, $90 - 65 = n$. The measure of $n$ is 25°.

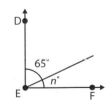

**Example:** If $\angle ABC$ is a straight angle (180°), what is the measure of $y$?

In this example, $36 + y = 180$. To find the missing angle measure $y$, subtract $180 - 36 = y$. The measure of $y$ is 144°.

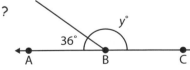

# Help Pages

## Solved Examples

### Geometry - Symmetry

A two-dimensional shape has a **line of symmetry** if it can be folded along a line into matching parts.

These shapes have one or more lines of symmetry .

These shapes have no lines of symmetry.

### Symbols

The ≈ symbol means "approximately equal to" or "about."  This symbol is often used when rounding and estimating.

Here is what the ≈ symbol would look like when rounding to the greatest place value:

$$\underline{3}4{,}142 \longrightarrow 30{,}000$$

or

$$3\underline{4}{,}142 \approx 30{,}000$$

Say, "34,142 is approximately 30,000" or "34,142 is about 30,000."

$$\underline{1}57{,}621 \longrightarrow 160{,}000$$

or

$$\underline{1}57{,}621 \approx 160{,}000$$

Say, "157,621 is about 160,000" or "157,621 is approximately 160,000."

# Help Pages

## Solved Examples

**Describing Patterns**

Patterns have shapes, numbers, or other items that either repeat or grow. The "rule" of a pattern describes HOW the pattern continues.

Study the pattern of shapes.

   The rule of this pattern is the circles alternate color (gray, white, gray, white, gray).

Study the pattern of numbers.

## 5, 10, 15, 20, 25

   The rule of the pattern is "Start at 5 and add 5 each time."

Sometimes the pattern is easy to see, but the rule is harder to describe.

Here is a pattern of triangles.

   The rule of the pattern is that the triangle rotates clockwise, 90 degrees each time.

Here is a pattern of numbers.

## 3, 13, 23, 33, 43

   The rule of the pattern is "Start at 3 and add 10 each time."

A "feature" of a pattern is another way to describe the pattern.

| Pattern | Rule | Feature |
|---|---|---|
| 5, 10, 15, 20, 25 | Start at 5; add 5. | All numbers end in 0 or 5. |
| 3, 13, 23, 33, 43 | Start at 3; add 10. | All numbers end in 3. |
| 7, 9, 11, 13, 15, 17 | Start at 7; add 2. | All numbers are odd. |
| 3, 8, 13, 18, 23, 28 | Start at 3; add 5. | All numbers end in 3 or 8. |

# Help Pages

## Problem Solving Strategies

### Make an Organized List

An **organized list** of possible answers for a problem uses an order that makes sense to you so that you do not miss any ideas or write the same answer more than once.

### Guess and Check

For the **guess and check** strategy, take a guess and see if it fits all the clues by checking each one. If it does, you have solved the problem. If it doesn't, keep trying until it works out. One way to know you have the best answer is when your answer fits <u>every</u> clue.

### Look for a Pattern

Sometimes math problems ask us to *continue a pattern by writing what comes next*. A **pattern** is an idea that repeats. In order to write what comes next in the pattern, you will first need to study the given information. As you study it, see if there is an idea that repeats.

### Draw a Picture

When you **draw a picture** it helps you see the ideas you are trying to understand. The picture makes it easier to understand the words.

### Work Backward

Using this strategy comes in handy when you know the end of a problem and the steps along the way, but you don't know how the problem began. If you start at the end and do the steps in reverse order you will end up at the beginning.

### Solve a Simpler Problem

When you read a math problem with ideas that seem too big to understand, try to **solve a simpler problem**. Instead of giving up or skipping that problem, replace the harder numbers with easier ones.

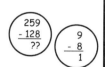

$$\begin{array}{r} 259 \\ -128 \\ \hline ?? \end{array} \qquad \begin{array}{r} 9 \\ -8 \\ \hline 1 \end{array}$$

### Make a Table

**Tables** have columns and rows. Labels are helpful too. Writing your ideas in this type of table (or chart) can help you organize the information in a problem so you can find an answer more easily. Sometimes it will make a pattern show up that you did not see before.

### Write a Number Sentence

A **number sentence** is made up of numbers and math symbols (+ − × ÷ > < =). To use this strategy you will turn the words of a problem into numbers and symbols.

### Use Logical Reasoning

**Logical reasoning** is basically common sense. **Logical** means "sensible." **Reasoning** is "a way of thinking." **Logical reasoning** is done one step at a time until you see the whole answer.

### Make a Model

A **model** can be a picture you draw, or it can be an object you make or find to **help you understand the words** of a problem. These objects can be coins, paper clips, paper for folding, or cubes.